May
H

May I
HELP YOU?

*great customer
service for
small business*

JILLIAN MERCER

ALLEN&UNWIN

First published in 2003

Allen & Unwin
83 Alexander Street
Crows Nest NSW 2065
Australia
Phone: (61 2) 8425 0100
Fax: (61 2) 9906 2218
Email: info@allenandunwin.com
Web: www.allenandunwin.com

National Library of Australia
Cataloguing-in-Publication entry:

Mercer, Jillian.
    May I help you?: great customer service for small business.

    ISBN 1 86508 858 7.

    1. Customer services. 2. Customer relations. 3. Small
    business. I. Title.

658.812

Set in 12/13pt Bembo by Midland Typesetters, Maryborough, Victoria
Printed by Griffin Press, South Australia

10 9 8 7 6 5 4 3 2 1

Contents

Acknowledgments

Many of my friends and colleagues are as passionate about customer service as I am. They often regale me at barbecues and social events with amazing, amusing and absolutely stupefying stories of bad service in businesses of all kinds. Although I often hear great stories of delivery of the best service in the most difficult circumstances as well, it was impossible to use them all for this book. However, my thanks go to Jennifer Binns, Sue Thompson, Ray Moss, Kimberley Heitman, Judith Morrisey and many others too numerous to list. Thanks also to small business owners such as Anita Verne, Steve Filmer and Marie Mercer.

My special thanks to Anne McKenzie, before whose skill and knowledge of customer service I stand in awe. She challenged me throughout the two major projects which have dominated this year, stopping me in my tracks if I became too complacent about the deeply complex and challenging issue of the service transaction. This book and my website, <www.nocustomerservice.com>, which is also based on the nine rules of good service, are far better for Anne's involvement.

Introduction

The importance of the service transaction

You already know what good customer service is about because every day in some way you are experiencing service as a customer—whether you are paying an electricity bill, going to the doctor or dentist, or buying clothing, a coffee or petrol. You may not be consciously aware of the service you are receiving, although if you give it some thought you will be able to discern what it is that made the experience either good or bad.

As a business person, if you have a burning passion for your business to do well, no matter what the business is, you will need to deliver excellent customer service. You can perform the customer service aspect of your business badly, in an average manner, or you can do it excellently. Do it excellently and your profits will soar.

Let me explain. Figure I.1 shows two boxes. Box number 1 represents your business and the work you do in either providing a tangible product or a service for which customers are prepared to pay. This book does not tell you how to run your business. Whether you offer a professional service, a trade, or are a small retail outlet, *you* have the expertise to run your business.

Box number 2 represents your customers. *They* know what their needs are, and you need to find out as much as you can about them. You may be able to guess what they want from you—especially in terms of your business practice. However, to know accurately, you need to ask them what they want from you in terms of service.

The gap between the two boxes represents the *service transaction*. This is where this book can provide valuable guidance through the nine rules of good customer service.

Figure I.1 The Service Transaction

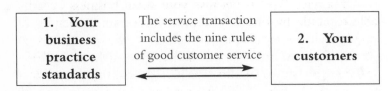

Your *business practice standards* relate to how well your business is run—how hot the food that you serve is, the quality of the widgets you manufacture, or how you otherwise conform to (or surpass!) accepted industry standards.

On the other hand, the *service transaction* is made up of nine specific rules that will help guide you to deliver the level of customer service that your customers have come to expect.

That gap between your business practice and your customers can seem very daunting and difficult to understand. It is often hard to separate our thinking about our business practice, as a photographer or a carpenter, for example, from the service practice in those businesses. How can this be done?

This book is designed to sort out the confusion between your business practice standards and your *customer service practice standards*. Often we are expert at our business practice standards and can't understand why our business doesn't seem to be doing that well. The secret is customer service. For your business to do well, you need both sets of practice standards working together to make sure your customers are happy to use your business, will tell their friends and colleagues about the experience and will use it again.

Each chapter of this book provides information on one of the nine rules necessary to understand just what is going on in that gap between your business practice and your customers.

The advantage of small business

The great news is that your small business has a distinct advantage over any large business when it comes to customer service. This is because your small business is easily able to abide by one of the most important principles of good service—*stay close to your customers*. The very nature of small business means you are already close to your customers and you can maintain that closeness. Large business is unable to do this easily and inexpensively. You're already there, close to your customers, and in the advantageous position of being able to hear what they want and what they don't like about doing business with you.

At the same time as enjoying the advantage of being close to your customers, you also face the overwhelming imperative that excellent customer service is even more important to your small business than it is to large businesses. This is because big businesses often have a large volume of customers, and subsequently good service practices are expendable as they can always rely on more unsuspecting customers to come along. Often this scenario can happen (and does!) because large businesses are monopolies in their business categories. Customers have no choice but to go to these big businesses and hand over their hard-earned money in return for the product or service they want.

Without your customers coming back, developing loyalty and being active word-of-mouth advertisements for your business, your business will fail. However, you *can* provide really good customer service, and this book will explain how.

Good customer service

There are some easy-to-remember ways of ensuring that the service you offer is the best available.

First, ask yourself this question: 'What is going on when I am receiving good customer service?'

Take a moment to answer yes or no, in response to the questions below:

- Were you greeted with a friendly smile?
- Was the salesperson helpful?
- Were you treated as if you were important?
- Were you given undivided attention during the service experience?
- Were there any unpleasant surprises?
- Was the business easy to use?
- Did the salesperson have good knowledge about the product you were interested in?
- Was the service fast?
- Was the service right the first time?
- If something went wrong, was it fixed quickly?
- Did the business follow up to check whether everything was in order?
- Was it easy to find out what you wanted and needed to know?
- Was it easy to understand how the business could serve you?
- Did the business let you know if it wasn't going to be able to meet its promises?

Are there other points that you can identify from your own positive experiences? What do you expect in terms of service in return for your business?

Look at the list again. These are the basics of good customer service. They represent behaviours which focus on the customer. The most important thing you can do for your customers is to ensure that, in every case, they have the same good experience when dealing with your business. Remember also that if these basics are not in place at your business, then at least *some* of your customers are experiencing bad service.

Trends in customer service

No matter how micro your business, or how specialist, you will be affected by emerging trends in customer behaviour.

Customers are becoming more educated, sophisticated, demanding, diverse, cash rich and time poor. At the same time, they are also becoming less patient, less loyal and less tolerant of low standards.

Customers are demanding higher standards than ever before. Now your suburban delicatessen is expected to serve coffees as good as the trendiest bar in the inner-city cappuccino strip—and with a more personalised service. If you're a tradesperson, you are expected to leave the work site in the same condition of cleanliness as the huge contracting companies that charge five times your rate per hour. It doesn't matter whether you are a plumber, carpenter or electrician, you are expected to provide good service in return for other people's hard-earned money. And, like doctors and other professionals, the new demands on your business will include making fixed appointments and keeping to them—no matter how impossible this may seem. If you provide accounting and financial services from a home office, your customers will demand the highest level of professional integrity and business knowledge, as they would from one of the big international business consultancy firms.

Contemporary customer service

High standards of customer service are within your control. The good news is that good customer service is just simple common sense. You *already* know a lot about customer service (just look at the number of times you answered 'yes' to the questions in the list above).

This book does not have any miracle solutions to make those 'pesky' customers go away. Nor does it provide you with a silver bullet to go straight to the heart of the matter. Instead, it provides nine guiding rules based on good, old-fashioned common sense, illustrated by examples of excellent practice. The service interactions are broken down into manageable parts to make it easier for you to understand how to tackle and improve components of your service effort with your customers.

Always remember the first principle of customer service: *stay close to your customers!* As we've established, you're already there because you are in a small business.

The next step is to learn and understand the nine guiding rules of good customer service as outlined in this book. The first rule sets standards which can be measured according to quality and accuracy. The other rules are guides and are more general in nature. The nine rules are:

- *Rule 1: Provide high standards of service.* High standards of service involve providing prompt service, asking customers for feedback, acting quickly and positively when things go wrong, always communicating effectively with your customers, being available to customers when they need you and making sure your customers only need to tell you what they want or need once.
- *Rule 2: Provide information to your customers.* Let your customers know in plain, simple and accurate terms about your business, what you can do for them, and how your services are run.
- *Rule 3: Be open and honest with your customers.* From the start, be very clear and honest about what your services cost, how well you perform them and who is in charge.
- *Rule 4: Offer choice to your customers.* Wherever possible, offer a range of options to your customers.
- *Rule 5: Consult with your customers.* Regularly and systematically ask your customers for their views about your service, then use this information to improve the service performance standards of your business.
- *Rule 6: Be courteous to your customers.* Ensure both you and your employees wear name badges, and that courteous service is *always* offered to every customer.
- *Rule 7: Be helpful to your customers.* Focus on helping customers and on meeting their needs and expectations. The convenience of your customers needs to be central, and services should be provided equally to all customers who are entitled to them.

- *Rule 8: Put things right for your customers.* When things go wrong, make sure customers are given a full explanation and offered an immediate apology, and that a swift and effective remedy is suggested. Implement a well-publicised and easy-to-use complaints process.
- *Rule 9: Provide value for money.* Deliver efficient and economical services to your customers.

This book will lead you through each of these guiding rules of good service. It offers both good and bad examples of businesses applying the rules. However, many of the guiding service rules are inextricably linked together. The book concludes with a chapter on managing complaints and 'customers from hell'.

chapter 1

RULE 1: PROVIDE HIGH STANDARDS OF SERVICE

The guiding rule when it comes to customer service is setting and maintaining high standards. These standards apply to all the rules discussed in later chapters, and for this reason some of those rules will be touched on here as well.

It is important to be able to measure the quality and accuracy of your service standards. This can be done by comparing them with those of your competitors, matching them to industry standards or looking at improvements and consistency in your own standards over time. Some of the aspects which can be measured easily are speed and accuracy. All the standards discussed in this chapter can be measured in one way or another.

A standard means the degree of excellence you want to achieve when it comes to customer service. The standards can be categorised under the following headings:

- *Prompt service*—providing efficient service to your customers, filling orders quickly, supplying information as soon as possible, answering the telephone promptly, making appointments for customers to minimise waiting times, removing extraneous and pointless tasks from your processes.
- *Convenience*—having opening hours which suit your customers, being available to hear complaints, offering a variety of ways of ordering or paying, ensuring your customers only have to make a request once.
- *Positive action*—dealing willingly with anything that goes wrong as quickly as possible.
- *Communication*—listening to your customers (especially when they have a concern), making sure customers

understand what you are saying, ensuring your message gets across to customers.

Providing prompt service

Customers today are more 'time poor' than ever before. They lead busy lives which makes it difficult for them to fit everything in. Your own life is probably busier than ever—indeed, the demands on you no doubt sometimes seem impossible. Remember that it is the same for your customers.

The speed with which you deliver service is important to your customers. Being forced to wait unnecessarily is a major source of irritation, and may result both in loss of business from customers who simply walk out and a subsequent decision not to return to your business in the future.

When your service processes are complicated and slow for the customer, you instantly create a difficult customer. The challenge for you—whether you're a plumber or a small retailer—is to speed up your service processes wherever and whenever you can: that's what providing prompt service is about. Some of the steps you can take to ensure service is delivered promptly are:

- Make it clear to customers how long they will have to wait for any service, and ensure you meet those times.
- Respond promptly to all telephone calls.
- Set specific appointments for your customers where relevant and apologise if your customers are kept waiting.

If you can't perform a service *every* time in a timeframe that meets the needs of your customers, it may be necessary to implement some process or system to let customers know that you are having problems, or that they may need to wait a little longer.

Speeding up your service

So how do you improve the speed of your service? This can seem very hard when you are already working to what you believe is your optimum output level. I recommend finding someone in the same business and watching how they manage *their* service transactions. If it isn't possible to watch, then become a 'customer' and try out their service. Observe every business you can and learn about the processes they use to deliver their products to the customer. This is a form of 'mystery shopping'—a way of learning how other businesses manage that gap between their business practice and their customers: the service transaction.

You need to learn everything you can about *efficient processes*. Take the ideas you observe in other businesses and copy them in your own. It doesn't matter if you are a mechanic and you get your ideas from the local beauty salon. Look for good ideas about managing processes and apply them to your business. In big business this is called 'process improvement'. Continually improving your processes by speeding them up will save time for both you *and* the customer. The unexpected benefit of process improvement is that you can also get rid of the absurd work that irritates you and wastes your time.

Absurd work

One of the easiest ways to speed up service is to remove *absurd work* from your processes. Absurd work is any unnecessary work you perform in your business that does not add any benefit or value to your business practices—a work process which is repeated day in and day out without making your business any better or faster. An example of absurd work would be constantly answering frequently asked questions such as 'When are you open?' The key to identifying absurd work is that it is often very irritating to perform. And if it is irritating you, it is probably irritating your customers as well! Absurd work is something that needs to be addressed, fixed up or removed from your practices. Frequently asked questions (FAQs) on company websites represent an attempt to remove absurd work from everyday activities. When you remove absurd work from your practices, it frees staff to give more attentive and focused service to your customers.

3

Slow service

Coffee shop blues

A good example of slow service speed can be found in a certain coffee shop franchise found in many countries in Asia and Europe. No matter how many people are in their shops, it always takes a long time to get a coffee. In some of their stores, queues of customers wait 30 minutes and more to get their orders (there is no table service). When I go for a coffee with friends I want to spend the time with them, not standing in a queue!

I maintain that there's something wrong with this coffee shop chain's processes. Other coffee shops can serve a coffee to a customer in seven minutes or less— regardless of how busy the shop may be (yes, I've used a stopwatch). They are all using the same coffee machines, so equipment can't be blamed. They are all facing the same vast range of customer requests for different beverages with accompanying foods, requiring different processing times—so where is the problem?

This service culture has been handed from franchise to franchise until it has become entrenched in the chain's business practice. The coffee shop franchise was once a small, one-shop business which grew into an international franchise. As the company has grown bigger, the capacity to stay close to its customers and serve their individual and special needs has diminished.

If I'm just one customer who won't go there because of the failure to provide prompt service, there will be others. And it is certain that those potential customers are also involved in bad word-of-mouth advertising that will eventually have an impact on the company's bottom line.

As a small business, you need to make sure that your customers only spread good word-of-mouth advertising. That's the best, cheapest form of advertising there is. The speed of your service is one of the elements that some customers will notice—and about which they will talk with their friends.

Answering the telephone promptly

A customer is anyone to whom you may provide a product or service of any kind. When the telephone rings, it will be a customer—or someone who might *become* a paying customer. If you fail to answer in a reasonable length of time, the customer at the end of the line will either hang up or be turned into an instant 'difficult customer'.

However, take care not to answer too quickly. Research by telecommunications companies around the world suggests that responding after three rings is a good standard. Too quick a response (one to two rings) can surprise customers and put them off their train of thought. You want them to feel very comfortable and welcome, so responding after three rings gives the customer time to adjust and get ready to communicate their requirements.

Never, under any circumstance, let a phone ring out. If you have regular periods when you know you are too busy with face-to-face customers, make sure you have an answering machine or message bank with an effective message recorded on it and switch the phone over to it. But make sure you phone the customer back as soon as possible.

Bad telephone practice

Recently, I had to attend an appointment at a medical specialist and was stuck in a queue in the carpark of the building, unable to get parking.

I tried calling from my mobile phone to say I was coming but would be some minutes late. Twice I tried and each time the phone rang out. The third time, someone picked up the phone and slammed it straight down—an action clearly designed to stop the insistent ringing—that my calls were causing at the other end. My fourth call was met by an engaged tone.

On arrival in the surgery, I noticed the phone was off the hook while the secretary/receptionist was engaged in some bookwork. I was kept waiting some 45 minutes for the specialist (another customer service issue). While

5

I was waiting, I noticed that the secretary occasionally put the phone back on the hook and as soon as it rang she either ignored or disengaged it.

This is appalling service practice and potentially very damaging for business. What's more, I've seen similar practices in hardware stores and takeaway food stores. There is no excuse for this sort of telephone service. Do that to your business and you will end up with customers who simply won't use your services—and the bad news about your business practice will quickly spread! Answering the phone promptly is a vital part of good customer service.

Better telephone practice

The medical receptionist in the above story was busy preparing some other work that was needed. However, there were alternatives she could have used, such as switching the phone over to take messages during that period.

But if you find you need to switch your phone over to your answering service all the time, and for periods as long as 30 minutes, you need to examine your business processes and find ways to make changes.

In this case, the owner of the business needed to be aware that this practice was occurring. Then the owner needed to work with the receptionist to find solutions to the situation.

A problem

One small Internet service provider company with which I worked was faced with the vexed question of what to do when the system went down for any reason. In such cases, the phone would ring hot with people wanting to know what was wrong and whether or not it was a system problem or a problem with their computer. The help desk staff would be inundated with the same questions and get exasperated giving the same answers. They would be unable to catch up, with callers banked up and getting angrier by the minute as the help desk system jammed with traffic overload. It became so bad that they were tempted to stop answering the phone. The transferred calls would also divert the technical people from being able to identify and work on the actual technical problem.

This was a very awkward situation which created very difficult, angry customers. What the customers experienced was both slowness in answering calls and slowness in informing them about what was going wrong with the system.

The solution

On analysis (by using a simple counting exercise), it became clear that there were only about half a dozen main reasons why the system might go down at the company's end. The answer to this problem could be found in the other good service rule of *informing your customers* (see Chapter 2). The company set up a pre-recorded message for each of the six possibilities. One message was very general and suggested that there was a technical problem and that staff were working on identifying it. As soon as the problem was identified, the first message would be removed and the appropriate message would be loaded into the system. This meant each customer who rang would be quickly, openly and honestly informed about the problem and the approximate time it would take to correct it. The new message system got rid of the absurd work of having to deal with phone callers who all had the same question and who all needed to have the same answer repeated to them. By sorting out the problem, the company was able to ensure prompt service—even during difficult times.

Complaints almost disappeared overnight once the system of messages was introduced to manage downtime. Staff no longer had to do the annoying absurd work of repeating the same information to customers who were also angry because they had been waiting in a jammed system.

The lesson here is that, if your business suffers regular,

7

intermittent rush periods when you are inundated with calls, implement a suitable way of dealing with them which avoids your customers being insulted, irritated or inconvenienced. Your method for dealing with the rush should inform the customers of why there are delays in an *open and honest* manner (see Chapter 3). Some of the other rules of good service have been utilised here to deal with the problem of a logjam of calls. The important thing is that there is *always* a better way to manage such a problem. You need to work out the way that best suits your business and also best matches your customers' needs and expectations.

To message or not to message
We know from all sorts of research about telephone message systems that customers always prefer to speak with a real person. The next best thing is a very good message system. Many people say they hate leaving messages, and there will always be some customers who feel this way. However, research also tells us that if you smile while you record a clear, friendly message, there is a greater chance that your customers will leave messages in return. This applies even to the most reluctant customers. There is a physiological explanation for this phenomenon: when we smile, the muscles that surround our voice box relax. The effect on our voice is that it sounds warmer and friendlier. This is why people who use their voices professionally, such as opera singers, speak with a slightly odd-looking smile on their face. When we leave a 'smiling' message, our customers can detect this and they respond accordingly.

Setting specific appointments for your customers

Your customers have busy lives, and need to plan their time. Effective management of your appointments benefits both you and your customers by making the most effective use of your time and theirs.

Setting specific appointment times for your customers relies on basic diary management. The story about the medical receptionist above leads on to the issue of appointments.

Hairdressers generally provide a good example of effective diary management. Their customers have varying needs, often without notice. Yet they seem to be able to organise their diaries. If you know a hairdresser, ask them how they work it out—then use the process in your business.

Good diary management

A dentist's main client base consisted of teachers. He offered good prices and discounts to encourage teachers to use him—it was his way of targeting a segment of his preferred customers who he knew were high-level users of dental services. Though his practice was in a capital city, many teachers from the country were his customers and naturally they needed their appointments in the school holidays. Although, like many health practitioners, he was often booked weeks and months in advance throughout the year, he had a very skilful way of managing his holiday diary.

He set aside at least half of each day in the school holidays (varying between morning and afternoon) and took advance bookings for the rest of those days. All the reserved times were held over and given only to those country callers who rang just a few days before the school holidays to make a booking. Some even waited until they had arrived in the city for the holiday break before calling to make an appointment. This ensured that, with minimum disruption, all of his customers were served appropriately during these times. The possibility of the times not being fully booked was taken care of because the country patients would often need several appointments. Everybody won!

The important thing is that this dentist knew his customer base and set up processes to meet *their* needs—not for his own convenience. He was a one-dentist, two-assistant practice that was doing very well and he managed the service standard of *providing prompt service* extremely well— despite the usual industry difficulties.

Know your customers' habits

The dentist was familiar with his customer base. As well, he knew how they tended to operate (ringing from the country very close to the time they needed the appoint-ment) and the times of the year they made their demands on his practice. Most importantly, he *adjusted* his business practices to *suit the needs of his customers*.

With doctors, many customers save up a list of little things that have been niggling them about their health, or know that they want to discuss a very worrying health issue. My local general practitioner has introduced a process of empowering his patients. When people ring to make an appointment, if they know they want to raise multiple issues with the doctor they are encouraged to ask the receptionist for a double appointment. There are clear, simply stated signs in the wait-ing room to inform patients of this and to encourage the practice. His appointments diary still gets out of control sometimes, but generally it has become much more manageable.

Research your customers' needs

Any professional or other personal service business can take similar action to sort out their appointments management. This is linked to *asking your customers what they want* (see Chapter 5).

In this situation, I always recommend some measurement. Count how many of your customers take longer than the standard time and measure how much time they actually take. Work that out across months, weeks and even days. Then arrange your appointments diary in the same way. Whenever the trends show a high number of long appointments, mark out your diary to have some hours per day when you see fewer customers. You may still come unstuck on some days, but don't let that divert you from your mission to get the appointments diary under control. Just keep observing and counting what is going on and make continual adjustments to your processes. This is the start of gaining control over the process of managing your appointments diary.

Tradespeople often lack skills in managing appointments

diaries. However, they too will better meet the needs of their customers if they have an effectively managed diary.

Many trades businesses only offer a half-day appointment window at best, refusing to make a specific appointment. This means customers have to arrange time off work to suit the convenience of the business. Invariably, these businesses also fail to offer weekend or after-hours appointments when the majority of people are home. This is often irritating and inconvenient for customers, particularly when the tradesperson fails to arrive at all and the customer has to take more time off work.

This business habit evolved at a time when there was usually someone at home during the day. But work patterns have changed radically and this is no longer the case. It is time for far better diary management in trades businesses.

The same situation applies to home deliveries of any kind. Deliveries after working hours and on weekends are now necessary to meet the needs of customers who either refuse or are unable to take time off work. Being able to make deliveries at set appointment times is an important part of good customer service.

Providing prompt service for your customers: questions for your business
- Does your business provide prompt service and responses to all your customers?
- Do you and your staff respond to customer requests promptly?

Practical tips for providing prompt service to your customers
- Answer all telephone calls promptly—no matter how busy you are.
- Implement a system of set appointments for customers, and practice good diary management of your appointments.
- Remove from your service practice absurd, repetitious work which slows your service down.

Convenience

Opening hours

Customers are demanding increased access to the goods and services they need. Even ten years ago, 24-hour, seven-day-a-week delicatessens, doctors' surgeries, dentists, hairdressers, restaurants and pizza delivery were inconceivable. Your opening hours therefore need to reflect the specific requirements of your customers—your services need to be available when your customers need them.

A friend of mine uses a mechanic in the outer suburbs. It is quite difficult to get there by public transport, making it difficult to deliver or collect the car during normal working hours. To assist customers, the mechanic is open from 7.00 a.m. to 6.30 p.m. each weekday and also on Saturday mornings so people can collect their cars at a time that suits them.

Consider shops that are closed on Saturdays and Sundays. How do customers who work the same hours as your business is open ever get to use them? You may be better off opening on Saturdays and closing on Mondays. Study and understand the peaks and troughs of customer traffic in your business and use that knowledge to maximise your customer service and therefore your profits.

As well as establishing opening times that suit your customers, it is important to be consistent. Even if it is quiet, it is vital that you open when you say you will. Use the quiet time to catch up on your bookwork and other tasks.

It takes time for customers to notice that you are open at different, more convenient times. You need to communicate the change in times and then give your customers the opportunity to get used to it. Customers need to know that your business will be open to serve them.

Staff availability

Many businesses—especially in retail—have full complements of permanent, knowledgeable staff in store on Monday mornings, the quietest time in retail. On Saturdays, when far more customers come to the stores, the tendency is to have casuals working who know less about the products and may be unfamiliar with service processes. If that is how your business is, reverse the trend. Have casual staff on duty at the quietest times and ensure all your permanent, knowledgeable staff are on duty during the busiest times.

Convenience: questions for your business
- Are you and your staff available to deal with customers' requests, issues and needs for service at times that best suit them?
- Are customers able to contact your business at times which are convenient for them?

Practical tips for being available to your customers
- Check with your customers that your opening hours meet their needs.
- Consider staggering staff duty hours so that you have staff on hand before and after ordinary working hours so customers can access your business outside their own work hours.
- Consider closing during quiet times (or operating with minimal staff) so you can be available when it is more convenient for customers to do business with you.

A single point of contact

In any business, it is important that a customer has to tell their story only once. Have you ever asked a question about an electricity bill, or tried to have a bank account sorted out? The more 'difficult' you are, the more people you seem to get passed on to. And each time you have to tell your story again, you feel more and more exasperated—you become a difficult customer. Make sure this never happens to *your* customers.

First, it is important that your customers have a single point of contact with your business. For this to work effectively, a single, named individual needs to be responsible for

13

ensuring your customers receive all the help they need from the very start of the transaction. The customer's story can then be passed around the business, where necessary, without the need for it to be repeated to every staff member encountered by the customer.

This good service standard also means ensuring that all staff in direct contact with your customers are fully trained and knowledgeable so they generally don't have to go to anyone else in the business to sort problems out.

Tracking systems

Second, processes need to be in place to ensure that you and your staff remember customers and their history with your business (both good and bad experiences). This means good tracking systems that any of your staff can access. These don't have to be expensive, sophisticated electronic systems. Good, well-designed filing systems can be just as good, and sometimes better—especially in small businesses. As well, good communication between staff means you can all be aware of the special needs and/or expectations of particular customers.

Some restaurants have simple, effective systems to track which food belongs to which person at which table. The system works because the table attendant assigns a number to each customer at a table. That number is then placed on the order next to each item ordered by that customer. Numbering is always done the same way (clockwise or counter-clockwise). But some restaurants still don't get it right and have staff standing at the top of the table yelling out 'Who's for the chicken?'

The important issue is that if any customer presents to your business, you must have error-proof ways of capturing all the relevant information you need to be able to serve them well; and it follows that that information is readily available at all times whenever that customer makes any contact with your business for any reason—no matter who actually serves them at any step in the service transaction process.

Mechanics can now create files for customers where every job done on a customer's vehicle is recorded along with the date. This means the mechanic can clarify when jobs were actually completed so the customer can work out whether there is a warranty involved, and when it is time to perform the service task again. Customers often have poor memories when it comes to this type of information. It helps your customers to know you have reliable records and builds customer confidence in your business—they feel you really do care about the history of their vehicle. To a customer, you aren't just concerned about completing the job quickly and getting paid for the work. The same applies to other services. Doctors, dentists, physiotherapists and hairdressers can all benefit from keeping track of their client's history.

Tracking over the long term

A friend's physiotherapist keeps such good records that he can tell his customers the last time they visited and exactly what it was for. He knows it takes about three years for my friend to get complacent about his back exercises. It is then that his old back muscle injuries are aggravated, and he ends up at the physiotherapist. It took six years for the physio to mention this (that's how long it took for him to be sure about the cycle of recurrence) and since then my friend has been able to manage his own condition better. If his old injuries start to niggle him, he gets diligent about his special exercises again to build his overall muscle strength. This means my friend needs to see the physio far less frequently, but he refers many of his friends to that physio because he knows he has the customer's best interests at heart. Certainly, the physio never has problems filling his appointments diary and employs three other professionals plus support staff in his two clinics.

Initial customer contact: questions for your business

- Are you and your staff able to capture each customer's story just once so customers don't have to keep repeating themselves?
- Do you and your staff have processes for tracking the background and details of each customer's history with your business?

Practical tips for providing a single point of contact for your customers

- Set up a simple system for keeping the relevant records of all your customers.
- Get some of your staff to specialise in an aspect of your business so they become your experts.

Positive action

This customer service standard has three aspects: providing the best possible service, with a positive, willing attitude; a high level of product or service knowledge; and being prepared to act immediately to solve a problem if one occurs. This final aspect is so important that it has been dealt with under Rule 8: *Put things right for your customers* (see Chapter 8).

What do customers want?

Customers want several distinct things from the service transaction. The first, and often most important, is a *relationship*. At the most basic level, having a relationship with your customer means:

- remembering and using their name;
- introducing yourself;
- wearing name badges to help them remember your name;
- remembering their history with your business; and
- remembering any special needs or preferences they have when doing business with you.

Many of these issues are discussed in this chapter, but they are often overlooked and it is important to remember them at all times.

The acronym CRM (Customer Relationship Management) is used in big business to describe this aspect of the service transaction with customers. Big business spends vast sums of money on electronic systems to capture all this information and have it readily available for all dealings with a customer. Despite the expense, the systems are not always effective, however.

There are several things other than a relationship that customers want from your business:

- getting it *right* first time;
- being *accessible* to customers;
- being *responsive* to customers;
- being *prompt* in responding to customers;
- having *knowledgeable* people serving customers;
- keeping customers *informed* about processes and what they can expect from us;
- providing any necessary *follow-up* on the product or service; and
- ensuring customers experience *no unpleasant surprises*.

These are all aspects of maintaining the highest possible standard of customer service. Sometimes things can go wrong, however, and the second aspect of good customer service is resolving these problems as quickly and effectively as possible by taking positive action. As this is dealt with in detail in Chapter 8, only a brief overview is provided here.

Taking positive action

Inevitably, things will go wrong and mistakes will be made in your business. Remember that if customers are complaining about mistakes, you should be looking hard at your business to see how you can rectify them. Don't bury your head in the sand and think you have a mistake-proof business. There is no such thing.

The most important thing is that you are able and willing to graciously, efficiently and effectively fix the problems when mistakes are made. The indicators that you are meeting this standard of good service are that:

- fast, effective and easy-to-use ways of putting things right are in place at each site for your business; and
- your staff respond positively when mistakes are made or services do not meet the standards your customers expect (and you advertise).

View complaints positively

Our natural tendency is to see the customer as a nuisance when they point out problems, rather than seeing them as a business asset. When a customer points out something that has gone wrong, it is a complaint—especially if there is a requirement for us to fix the mistake or respond in some way.

When a customer complains, they are helping your business by pointing out what needs to be done differently to improve your business. They are helping you to recognise where things are going wrong, where errors are occurring and where mistakes are being made. If you really listen to your customers, you may even find that there are some service black holes where more things go wrong than in your other business process areas.

By focusing on fixing the problems highlighted by customers, you are utilising very inexpensive consultancy advice to make your business better.

Rapid complaints management

When things go wrong, it is important to fix the mistake with the minimum of fuss. There are three simple steps to take immediately:

1 *Apologise.* Tell the customer you're sorry this happened.
2 *Thank* the customer for pointing out the error/mistake.
3 Work out how to *rectify* the problem in the simplest,

fastest way, and let the customer know you regard this as a priority.

This method comes from American customer service consultant Mary Gober. Her method for rapid complaints management (which she refers to as the Sorry–Glad–Sure, or SGS, method) is based on what customers feel when they make a complaint: first, they want empathy and acknowledgment that something has gone wrong; second, the customer will feel immediately acknowledged and less aggrieved if you thank them for pointing out the error; and finally, they want to know that the problem will be fixed quickly, with the least possible expense and disruption to their life.

Managing complaints is a very complex and challenging task, and for this reason it has been dealt with in more detail in Chapter 8.

Putting things right for your customer

A successful small business plumber who employed ten certified tradesmen and three apprentices told me about a single mother who worked for ten years to save every cent she could towards the building of her small, modest dream home. A relative had given her a set of gold-plated kitchen taps as a gift. These were to be the centrepiece of the modestly grand kitchen that had been cooked up in the dreams of this young woman. There was just one problem: once the kitchen was all fitted out with cabinets and appliances, the gold taps looked all wrong. It was a design and style error that even her primary school-aged children noticed and teased her about. With all the stress of the moment, our young mother ended up on the phone crying to the plumber because she simply did not have a spare cent to do anything about replacing the taps with more appropriate ones.

This wasn't even a complaint as such, because the plumber had done nothing wrong. However, he offered to replace her taps and have the new, simpler chrome ones fitted at no extra cost (he absorbed the labour costs). The customer was absolutely delighted. The total cost to the plumbing business was $150, but he considered it an investment in advertising. Within three months, he had received actual contracts from four other customers, each of whom had been referred by this single mother in distress.

Efficient customer service: questions for your business

- Do you and your staff build and maintain a relationship with the customer?
- Do you and your staff fix mistakes with the minimum of fuss each and every time they occur?
- Do you and your staff apologise immediately when things do go wrong?
- Do you and your staff immediately provide full explanations to customers in the event that things go wrong?
- Do you and your staff agree to fix problems immediately when things do go wrong?

Practical tips for taking positive action when things go wrong for your customers

- Understand that mistakes will happen and errors will occur in your business—and help your staff to understand this as well.
- Institute a policy of thanking the customer immediately when they point out where things have gone wrong in the service transaction.
- Make sure you and your staff fix all problems immediately or as soon as possible once you become aware of them.
- Always aim for a positive, win/win solution (for you and the customer) when things go wrong.

Communication

If there is one aspect of customer service that is most important—and also most neglected—it is *communication*: making contact with your customers, listening to them (especially when they have a concern), making sure customers understand what you are saying and ensuring that *your* message gets across to your customers.

Greeting your customers

Courtesy is crucial. A customer who is greeted enthusiastically and courteously from the beginning of the business transaction will immediately warm to you and your business.

The proprietor of a small restaurant I often go to always personally greets every group of customers with a warm welcome and a quick chat. Needless to say, his attention to individual customers is only part of the service. The result of this small but important gesture is that his business is booming.

Informing your customers

Providing information to customers is crucial to customer service. Without information, they are unlikely to use your business, especially to its full potential. This aspect of customer service is dealt with in detail in Chapter 2.

Communicating effectively

When dealing with your customers face-to-face or in writing, they must easily understand the language you use—it must be tailored to their needs. The indicators of performing this standard well in your business are:

- Your customers can easily find out everything they want to know about your business services and products because of clear and effective communication.
- You communicate this information in writing where possible.

There is a small inner-city Asian supermarket near my home. It stocks everything needed for Asian cooking, including imported and locally grown perishables. The signs for each of its product aisles are simplicity itself. Each has the general items in four languages: English and three Asian languages representing the main customer segments of the store. They have been neatly done in handwriting on pieces of coloured cardboard—easy to do, easy to read and cheap to produce. Like this shop, your effective communication doesn't have to be elaborate or expensive.

Using your customers' language

A roadhouse owner on an isolated country highway complained about the 20 or 30 'stupid' customers per day who would walk into his very busy roadhouse and ask things like 'Where are your drinks?' This was despite the fact that, directly in front of the main entrance through which the customer had walked, sat a huge fridge containing all the drinks, which was largely, glossily sign-posted 'REFRESHMENT CENTRE'.

His customers were using the word 'drinks' to him, but he was using the phrase 'refreshment centre'. My advice to him was to get a big piece of butcher's paper (anything) and a big black marker pen, write the word 'DRINKS' on it, tape it over 'REFRESHMENT CENTRE' and see what happened.

The problem all but disappeared overnight because the sign was effectively communicating in the language the customers used and could relate to.

A key to establishing whether or not your communication is effective is if you or your staff start hearing yourselves calling the customers 'dumb' or 'stupid' because they 'just don't understand!' If your customers don't understand, it is because you are not *communicating effectively* about what it is you need them to know or to do. It is your responsibility as a small business owner to communicate in a way which works so that your customers know what is expected of them.

It is also very important to be open and honest with your customers at all times. If you cannot meet deadlines, have a limited range, or there are additional fees, customers should know about it at the start of the transaction. This aspect of good communication is dealt with in Chapter 3.

Effective communication: questions for your business

- Do you and your staff use language to help your customers understand what is going on with your business and its products?
- Does all the written material in your business use clear and simple language which is easy to understand?

Practical tips for communicating effectively to your customers

- Ask some trusted customers whether they understand your written material (including signs, directions, instructions for use, brochures, process descriptions).
- Keep your communication simple and to the point to make it easy for customers to understand your business and how it works for them.
- Examine your business premises like a stranger would. Start from the front of the building or office/shop space and make a list. What do you see which is good and bad, or off-putting? What should you change?
- Mystery shop your own business with a new staff member or a stranger. Try to experience what it is like to visit your business for the first time.

Asking your customers

Communication is a two-way affair, and this aspect of good customer service involves asking your customers what they think about your service—again, and again, and again.

Many large businesses actually hire actors to play the role of customers who go into their shops and assess the performance against a list of criteria to do with their interpretation of service standards. This is called 'mystery shopping'. But in small business you don't need to go to the expense of hiring 'mystery shoppers' because you are already so close to your customers. You can ask them yourself—and at no cost except a bit of time and the added bonus of contributing to the building of a relationship with them.

There really are only three questions you need to ask your customers. Those questions are:

1 What do we do badly?
2 What do we do well?
3 What do we need to do differently to make it easier for you to be our customer?

This aspect of customer service is dealt with in more detail in Chapter 5.

Asking your customers: questions for your business

- Do you ask your customers for feedback before making decisions about changes to service practices?
- Do you ask your customers what they think is the one thing you should improve about the way you serve them?
- Do you and your staff ask your customers what their priorities are for service delivery?

Practical tips for asking your customers

- Ensure you ask one customer per week what you could do differently to make it easier for them to be your customer.
- Change your service processes to match the suggestions from your customers.

Overview

This chapter has focused on high standards of service, in the areas of convenience, efficiency and communication. These standards are mainly about speed and efficiency—and they can be measured so you can judge how well you are performing them.

The good service rule for providing high standards of customer service is about the efficiency with which you manage the service transactions in your business. If your business is really efficient in the eyes of your customers they will notice that you consistently:

- offer prompt, efficient service;
- respond quickly to customers, both in person and on the telephone;
- remove absurd work from your processes;
- wherever possible, make set appointments for your customers;
- open for business at times that suit your customers;
- have experienced staff on hand at busy times who know your business, its services and products;
- take immediate positive action when things go wrong, and fix any problems quickly and effectively;
- communicate effectively with your customers by using language that they can understand when dealing with them face-to-face or in writing;
- provide a single point of contact for your customers and ensure that they do not have to tell their story to you more than once;
- keep good records of your customers' history with your business.

Business transactions rely not just on one standard of good customer service, but on a combination of many of these standards. The emphasis should always be on striving to perform each of them as effectively and willingly as possible.

chapter 2

RULE 2: PROVIDE INFORMATION TO YOUR CUSTOMERS

Providing information to customers is one of the most important rules of good service. Your customers need adequate information about every aspect of your business that affects them. The challenge is to ensure you provide adequate information about the right things. This means not leaving your customers feeling inundated, but rather that they are fully aware of what your business is all about.

You know your business is performing well on this rule of good service if it readily provides to your customers full, accurate information in plain language about:

- your business;
- what you can do for them; and
- how your services are run.

A failure to provide adequate information is almost a guarantee that you will turn ordinary customers keen to purchase from you into difficult customers who will be reluctant to give you anything. No one wants to deal with difficult customers if it can be avoided, and one of the best ways to avoid it is to ensure they have all the information they need to make it easy for them to do business with you.

This rule of good service is linked to the standard of being open and honest which was raised in Chapter 1 and is discussed in more detail in Chapter 3.

Customers don't understand

Every time you have heard a staff member (or yourself) say 'the customer didn't understand' or 'the customer didn't listen' you can be sure that you have not provided adequate information for that customer about your business—or an aspect of it.

Whenever a customer presents as 'not knowing' or 'not understanding', it is probably because you have not explained adequately or provided enough of the *right* sort of information.

The customer's perception is 100 per cent correct: a person's perception is simply how they see things. This is the basis of the old adage that 'the customer is always right'. If there is a gap between what the customer is perceiving and what you know to be the facts about your business, then it is up to you to inform the customer so they have a more accurate understanding of the situation. It is *your* business and it is your responsibility to work with the customer so that they understand and are therefore more likely and willing to give you their hard-earned money.

What information is the right information?

Customers need many kinds of information about your business in order to do business with you. Such information includes:

- services you provide;
- how your business processes work;
- expected process times;
- opening times and hours;
- internal signage;
- costs and charges.

Services you provide

If customers know what you can do for them, they are likely to return. They will also use more of your services, enabling you to build that all-important *relationship with the customer*. Ultimately, you want each customer to return regularly. So it is important to make them aware, as soon as possible, of all you offer in the way of services.

27

Because our lives are getting busier and busier, it is critically important that, where possible, you provide services that save time for your customers. These may include the following:

- special deals to save money;
- home delivery;
- carrying large purchases to the customer's car;
- accepting orders for services or products via fax;
- wrapping purchases for presentation as a gift;
- providing electronic funds transfer;
- dealing directly with insurance or other agencies on behalf of customers.

Special deals to save money
Deals available to customers may include discounts for bulk purchases, or the availability of loyalty programs to encourage customers to return to you as the preferred business. No matter what your business is, you will have various special services that you offer and are prepared to deliver for your customers (whether in retail, in the trades, or in the professions). Let your customers know about them.

Home delivery
Delivering products to people is a fantastic service, particularly for people who can't get around easily, such as senior citizens or people with disabilities. If you provide a home delivery service or service in their homes, make sure you let your customers know. Generally customers will not mind paying a little more for this service, but it is important to tell them about the extra cost at the beginning.

Carrying large purchases to the customer's car
Carrying large, bulky or heavy purchases to your customers' cars is a great service and a great way to build gratitude in your customers—and gratitude leads to loyalty. For many customers—from busy, harassed parents with toddlers through to disabled people or the elderly—it is invaluable to have someone help them to the car with a purchase.

Never begrudge this service, no matter how busy you are. Always offer it to anyone who even vaguely looks like they might appreciate the help, and make sure you let your customers know this service is available.

Accepting orders for services or products via fax

If you are flexible in the way you can receive orders, tell your customers about it. One example is a small catering company which offered phone-based service to some of its customers who were disabled and unable to get out of their cars with ease to pick up their orders. The customer would telephone the order in and arrange the time for pick up. Then, as the customer was nearing the shop, they would use their mobile phone to ring through to the shop that they were arriving. The staff would then take the product out to the entrance and complete the transaction there.

The business found that its customers were telling all their friends who had similar difficulties with shopping, and they were using the service as well. It could be argued that the level of service required for such transactions is too high. However, in the process the shop built a huge amount of loyalty and respect from the friends of these customers who were not themselves disabled and who used the more conventional service processes.

Wrapping purchases for presentation as a gift

Customers love to take away a purchase which is wrapped in beautiful paper and which looks special. If such a service is appropriate to your business—for example, selling jewellery or lingerie—offer it and let your customers know.

Providing electronic funds transfer

Providing options for payment to your business is a good customer service practice. Customers have differing preferences for how they like to pay for services and products—and their preferences may change.

Direct debiting of bank accounts (or electronic funds transfer) is a cheap and economical way to move money directly out of a customer's bank account into yours. Both your customer and your business win if you offer this service, and its availability will both attract more customers and encourage them to spend more money with your business.

Dealing directly with insurance or other agencies on behalf of customers

In many areas, such as health and ancilliary service provision, customers have insurance cover to assist with the payment of their accounts. It is common practice now for such businesses to offer a service where insurance rebates can be claimed electronically and instantly from the insurer, leaving just the gap for the customer to pay. This puts less strain on the customer's finances and also saves them having to go to the insurer to claim the rebate. If you offer direct deduction from third parties, make sure you inform your customers.

How your business processes work

It is important for customers to understand how the processes affecting your service to them work. For example, if your business is in a rural or isolated area and you know that certain parts or products must always come from distant cities or even other countries, you need to state this up front at the beginning of the transaction. Likewise, if there are regular delays for any reason, you also need to make this clear to customers. With this understanding, they are less likely to become difficult customers.

Providing information to customers ensures they experience no surprises—especially unpleasant ones. This rule also applies if forms have to be filled in before the next step in the process can occur. You must let your customers know this at the start of their transaction with you.

Expected process times

You should know how long it takes to do almost everything in your business because it will effect your customers. You can then keep your customers informed about how long they might expect to wait for any aspect of the service transaction.

Inform your customers about any excessive waiting times and provide reasons. Also explain if the service is speedier than usual. Customers are busy (just as you are) and unexplained waiting times are a major irritation.

For example, in a restaurant, if a special dish requires extra cooking time, it should be noted on the menu next to the dish entry. The customer then has the opportunity to choose another meal. On the other hand, if your business deals with takeaway food, let customers know how long it will be before their meal is ready. This avoids waiting and irritation, or cold food.

If you are a doctor or other service or medical professional, let clients know about particularly busy times. They can then decide whether to choose another time when they won't have to wait so long. Or they can be prepared with a book to read, or some other activity to fill in time while they wait.

Opening times and hours

Information about opening times needs to be consistent and reliable. Do you have customers turning up at odd times and displaying irritation about your inaccessibility? It may be an indication that you are not being clear about the times you are available and/or open for business. In my training sessions, I often ask the staff of businesses: 'What bugs you about your customers?' In one company, the staff said that having to repeatedly tell people opening times really irked them. There are several ways to sort this problem out:

- Have clear, simple 'opening times' signs displayed around the building.
- Print up a simple 'opening times' leaflet to hand to customers if they ask the question.
- Have a little stand of cards/bookmarks with the opening times on them.

These are simple, inexpensive solutions which can have a big impact on getting rid of most of the 'absurd' work in this instance. Remember, absurd work is the repetitive work that doesn't add any value to the services or processes of the business. In fact, absurd work usually slows you down—but it's work nonetheless.

Internal signage

Internal signage is extremely important for guiding your customers through a hassle-free experience with your business. To understand how important signage is, just go to a large complex like a university, a hospital or a shopping centre that you have never visited before. Notice how difficult it is to find where you need to go! Some large organisations do signage well; others fail dismally.

Even in a small business, be scrupulous about making sure your signage is accurate and clear. Watch your customers enter your shop and observe how they cast their eyes around looking for what they want. Be wary of presenting trendy signs in funny colours and patterns at heights at which humans do not normally look. The aim of signage is to help your customers *independently* find what they are looking for in the simplest, fastest way—ideally, without having to come to you or your staff for assistance. Also make sure your signs are clear, simple and to the point.

Costs and charges

Customers need to be aware of all costs involved in a transaction. To begin with, it is important to inform customers about the base charges for your services and products. Then they need information about any additional costs and charges they can expect to pay at all stages of the service transaction.

Make sure all your products or services are clearly labelled with prices so the customer can see them. Some sales technique trainers assert that it is better not to have prices marked so that the customer is forced to ask for the price. With this method, you get the opportunity to engage with them and do a 'sell job' on them. However, this can be very irritating if a customer just wants to do a quick check and comparison. It is better to ignore the sales technique advice and concentrate on improving the service by ensuring that prices are clearly displayed.

Listen to your customers

Listening skills are vital when it comes to providing information to your customers. It is important to find out where you can provide information, as well as how much and what kind of information the customers want. This rule is related to *consulting with your customers* (see Chapter 5). Listen to what your customer does not understand and check with them about what they need to know.

When a customer obviously doesn't understand something and keeps asking for an explanation, it is because you are not explaining the issues in a way that they can understand. Explain the process or the information again, in a manner that better fits the customer's needs—which may differ from the way you *think* it should be communicated.

Remember that you are the expert in your business, but the customer is the expert when it comes to what they want to meet their needs and expectations. Your skill must be in bridging the gap between the two, and that gap is where the service transaction takes place. Your business needs the customer to be fully informed so that they feel comfortable dealing with you and confident that they have the knowledge to make the decision to purchase your product or service.

Put yourself in the customer's position to understand their perspective. Then decide how much and what type of information you need to provide to them. Don't fall into the big-business trap of assuming that all customers are the same, wish to be treated the same and therefore require the same information. It is a constant challenge to keep on evolving to meet the varying needs of each and every customer. Some aspects can be standardised, such as signage. However, at the face-to-face level, after providing certain basic information, you will need to constantly monitor the customer to decide what level of information you will provide to them. 33

Overview

Your customers need you to provide good, appropriate and useful information so that they can understand your business, making it easy for them to be your customers. This rule of good service, *providing information to your customers*, is about ensuring that you keep your customers well informed about the service standards they can expect and that you can provide. You know your business is performing well on this rule of good service if you can confidently say that you readily provide to your customers full, accurate information in plain language about your business, what you can do for them and about how your services are run.

You need to ensure that all key areas relevant to your business customers are effectively dealt with.

Providing information to customers: questions for your business

- Does your business provide full and accurate information in plain language to help customers understand your business and services?
- Do you and your staff clearly state service costs so that customers can easily understand them?
- Do you use plain language in all communications to customers?
- Do you adhere to the costs and charges you advertise?

Practical tips for providing information to your customers

- Make sure you have good, simple information available about your services and products and any rules you have about how your customers can engage with you.
- Check with your customers to make sure you provide the right amount of information.
- Ask a trusted customer, and a new one, what they

think your business can do for them. If they miss anything, make sure you design a way to inform your other customers about the service.

- Stop yourself and your staff in the middle of saying 'the customer doesn't understand'. Then work out *what* it is they do not understand and find a way to better inform the customers about it.

chapter 3

RULE 3: BE OPEN AND HONEST WITH YOUR CUSTOMERS

It is important for your small business to be open and honest with your customers about your limitations and any problems you may have in providing service.

You will earn your customers' respect and loyalty by being honest about your business capabilities and limitations. This means ensuring that information about your products and services, including pricing structures, is readily available to your customers in plain language from the start. This standard of good service makes it easy for your customers to do business with you.

Implement this standard by providing clear information, in the form of signs and/or leaflets, about:

- pricing structures and charges including:
  - aspects of service where extra charges automatically apply;
  - discount circumstances where discounts are available and the conditions for receiving them;
- times you are open for service;
- normal waiting times for services;
- any expected and regular delays in delivery;
- any unexpected mishap that will affect service or supply in the short term;
- follow-up service which is provided;
- rules or policies affecting the service your customers will receive;
- options for making complaints to you if some aspect of the service transaction has gone wrong;
- all the products you are able to supply;

- any services or products you do not, choose not, or are unable to supply; and
- regular busy times when service turnaround might not be up to your usual standards.

The 'small print' in insurance documents and contracts is a classic example of avoiding full disclosure. Notice whether customers react negatively to or are surprised about some aspect of your business delivery. If you think you can't detect any examples, ask a couple of loyal customers whether there were any unexpected and unpleasant surprises the last time (or any time) they did business with you. If so, ask what they were.

If there are any hidden costs involved in changing an order, make this clear to customers, and explain exactly when extra costs will be imposed.

Quotes

Quoting is one area where being open and honest is important. Always give realistic quotes, but if you find you can't do the job for less than you have quoted, be open and honest about it as soon as possible. As well, make sure that your quotes detail all aspects of the job, with a clear statement of the cost of each segment of the quote. With quoting, it is better to give more detail than less. Your customer may well have a contact in the same industry with a good knowledge of rates and charges. Your chance to win the contract for a job may be destroyed over a family barbecue where you can't even defend your quote and the service you offer.

Plumb dumb

I sought three quotes from plumbers to complete a large job on a home I was renovating. One quote came in at 30 per cent higher than all the others. When I questioned the plumber, he assured me that quality of service was higher from his small business than the other quoters and that, among the benefits of using his business, he would 'do the job right first time'. I decided to go with him for these reasons as the work was complex and I wanted it to be as worry-free as possible.

As he was to install plumbing for two bathrooms, two toilets, a full kitchen and laundry, plus front and rear outdoor taps and all drainage, I felt confident I had chosen the right company.

Yet I had to call him back five times to fix even the most basic of problems. Once, when I rang him, he became angry and complained that 'you can't trust anyone any more and that the apprentice (!) had not done his job properly!'

Apprentice? I thought I was getting the highest quality service from highly qualified and experienced professionals. This was a company that had promised the highest quality of tradesmanship and service.

Fortunately, I was able to request an inspection by a government water authority inspector at no cost. The water authority inspector found many very basic faults with the whole plumbing job (including an overflow pipe under one bathroom floor that was not connected to the drainage system). As you can imagine, this was not what I had expected with a job costing 30 per cent more than quoted by other contractors.

Broken rules

So what were the broken rules in this example?

First, the plumber failed to be open and honest about *who* would do the job—he later admitted that an apprentice did most of the work. Second, he didn't take positive action when things went wrong (Rule 1)—and he certainly didn't offer an apology. Finally, because of all the other things that were wrong, the service speed was slowed right down (Rule 1).

Cost of services

People need to know the cost of doing business with you. And they want to know earlier rather than later.

Price is a key differentiator between businesses. However, most people who can afford to will pay a premium price if they feel the product and the service match the price. The important thing is to tell customers about the cost of your goods and services as soon as possible. It is also important to ensure there are no nasty surprises down the track.

Being open and honest about the cost of your services is different from providing value for money in that it is about providing *information* to your customers about prices and costing structures.

For example, some restaurants have photos of their standard meals displayed with prices on them. As soon as you enter, it is clear that you can purchase specific food items for set prices. Signs often explain circumstances where the price may vary—for example, when a particular food (e.g. avocado) is in season, or if any condiments are to be added to a meal.

However, too many options can be confusing. It is best to keep fees and charges as simple as possible—and be open about them.

Rates and charges

Professional service industries often have a poor record when it comes to being open about rates and charges. After seventeen years of using the same accountant, my friend Bill still doesn't know what the price structure is. Each year when the accountant's invoice arrives, he is unpleasantly surprised. However, such practice seems endemic in the industry. Even if Bill changes his accountant, there is no guarantee that he will find an accountant who is open about rates and charges. This is ironic, because accountants are, after all, in the business of measuring and understanding the value of money.

Providing fixed quotes

This lack of information about pricing structures is also common in the health industry. In many countries, there have been attempts to make practitioners more account-able, with the result that dentists and other health practi-tioners provide fixed, itemised quotes for all work to be performed, including complex and lengthy procedures. In many industries, just broadcasting an hourly rate would be a good start.

Flexible hourly rates?

A friend started her own micro business as a manage-ment consultant. She decided on a realistic fee that would both cover her on-costs and be relatively competitive with other providers in her area of expertise. The advantage of a set rate for all work meant that it was very easy to give quotes quickly and efficiently. Shortly after she set up her business, she was approached by several companies to form a partnership. A representative from one company asked what she expected to charge, and she quoted her set hourly rate. He became quite conspiratorial, dropped his voice and said: 'But what if you can get away with charging more to those that can afford it?' My friend was taken aback. She immediately decided against working with them because she was uncomfortable about operat-ing without standard, well-publicised rates and charges that were fully understood by her clients.

Advantages of set rates

If you do have set rates, it is much easier to be open and honest about your charges for any job. Remember that *you are the expert in your field*. You should have a reasonably accurate idea of how long it takes you to perform any of your business processes. If you have a standard rate for tasks and jobs, then it is much easier to give efficient and reasonably accurate quotes to your customers. You know how long each job should take; you know the standard rate; and by combining this knowledge you are in a position to give your customers speedy, accurate information about costs.

Discounts

A retailer in a country town told me he offered reduced rates for his special customers—those who purchased large volumes of products. But word got out that he only offered these substantial discounts to *some* customers. The problem was that some of his other regular customers heard about the discounts and wanted them too. When he asked how he could sort the problem out, I told him he needed to be open about his discounting practices. That meant having a brochure or signs in his shop advising all his customers about the quantities needed to receive a discount. His main problem was not that he gave discounts, but that he often simply gave them to his friends on a whim: his discounting policy was inconsistent.

Hidden charges

Customers like to know the total cost of goods or a service up front. Don't use some kind of 'small print' to hide costs. If your business involves any sort of value-added tax, all your prices must include the tax.

Standardised fees and charges

As well, you may need to simplify your charges and fees so that they are more standardised. This is difficult if you are in a highly price-sensitive and competitive market. However, as discussed in Chapter 9, dealing with *value for money*, some customers are willing to pay a premium price if the product or service is supported by premium service. In this instance, by simplifying and standardising your costing and charges, you can be very clear about what services and products cost and then clearly and unambiguously communicate this to your customers.

Last-minute surprises

A friend rang me one day, very angry about service she had received from a motor mechanic. She had taken her car for a service that she understood would cost her about $300.

After work, she went to collect the car and was told that the cost was actually $800—an amount she had to pay immediately in order to collect her car. The garage had failed to call her to let her know that, while working on the car, they had found some additional problems. None of them would have caused immediate danger to her as the driver and each problem could have been addressed at a later stage. As well, the mechanic failed to ask my friend how she would like to deal with further repairs. As it was (see Chapter 5, on *consulting your customers*), she was embarrassed because she had budgeted for a lesser amount and had insufficient funds to cover the repair bill. This was a classic case of hidden or further costs not being revealed until late in the transaction.

Hiding, or neglecting to communicate, information about prices is a classic example of how to create a difficult customer. Customers understand that they have to pay for products and services. If, during the transaction, the customer says they want extras or other services or products, then let them know at each point about the costs involved. Have brochures that clearly explain how your cost structures work so that your customers will know when the price will change.

Hidden costs can provide unpleasant surprises in a whole range of trades and professional service areas. Other examples of what not to do include:

- offering to gift wrap a purchase and then adding the charge on without letting the customer know;
- in restaurants, charging 'corkage' per person at the table whether they are drinking or not; and
- offering to deliver a product, only to reveal a hefty delivery fee at the last minute.

If you have ever opened an invoice and been unpleasantly surprised about the amount, the service provider has not been open about pricing structures and policies. Ensure that this never happens to any of *your* customers.

Performance of services

Being open and honest also extends to your service—to how well you perform a task. That means not taking on work you are not qualified or capable of handling. It is much better for your reputation to say that a job is out of the ambit of your business and to offer an alternative in the industry than to take on a job, fail to meet customer expectations and end up with bad word-of-mouth advertising.

Stick to your 'knitting'

Some small businesses 'stick to their knitting', which means they only take on work they know they are really good at. This means the business always delivers on time, within budget and with the room to deliver excellent service to customers. As well, in the spirit of openness, they always tell the inquiring customer *why* they don't do the specific work or carry the specified product required by the customer.

In order to be even more helpful to customers, they maintain a list of businesses and service providers in similar industries that may specialise in the aspects of the industry they don't handle. The customer is grateful to end up with a supplier who can serve their specific needs.

Some retailers, such as pharmacies, claim a product size or type is not available because they don't stock it. This is very poor practice at best, and often an outright lie. Customers usually make specific requests because they are familiar with and prefer a particular size or variation of product or service. It is better to say: 'That product does exist; however, we don't stock it and/or the alternative we have or can offer you is . . .' Most customers will accept an alternative and respect your openness. If you say the product doesn't exist—

even if it is because you just don't know about it—the customer will not only realise that you are less knowledgeable than them, but will feel you are implying they are a liar—one easy way to lose a customer forever.

Selective tendering

Many small businesses, from builders through to caterers, do what is called selective tendering. This means they choose carefully which jobs they will take on. While this may seem contrary to the notion of taking on any job to build your business, taking on a job for which you are not adequately trained or equipped is potentially very damaging to your business.

It is better to concentrate on those jobs you know you are really good at and build your business from that very sound foundation. You can then advertise your business accordingly, telling customers that you are the best/fastest/most qualified to perform particular aspects of your business.

Keeping promises

It is important to have a good understanding of your service and business standards. This means that you can tell your customers reasonably accurately how long it will take to perform certain services, and the quality they can expect. If you are selling a product rather than a service, it means being very clear and honest about the capabilities of the product.

Remember, your customers are not fools. They will soon realise that you are not up to standard as soon as you start to break promises or botch the service transaction. If you are honest about your limitations, they will respect you; if not, they will no longer trust your business.

Local area advertising

For many years I owned and drove a very old English sports car. Over that time, I had many jobs done and redone on the car. Where possible, I prefer to buy local to assist local commerce. For this reason, I started using a local panelbeater for general body maintenance on the car. I'm no expert about panelbeating, but I did expect that basic competence would prevail. However, after he had completed about four small jobs (for example, cutting out rust spots) over as many years, I started to get comments from other experts in the motor vehicle industry about the poor quality of the work. When I tackled the panelbeater about the workmanship (on jobs which were rapidly disintegrating, and which had to be redone), he just said to me: 'But I'm the cheapest in the industry!' It was only then that he was honest with me about his business practice parameters!

With *caveat emptor* [buyer beware] in mind, I ought to have been a more discriminating customer and sought other quotes. However, if he had been honest, he'd have needed a sign saying: 'We're not good, but we're cheap'. No business in their right mind would do such a thing, but he was already saying it with his business practice, and his ex-customers and other industry operatives were saying it for him too. Local area mechanics and others actively recommended that people not go to him. It was amazing how he had organised a very skilful network of advertisers against his business without even realising he was doing it!

Our erstwhile panelbeater is not in the local area any more. He's had to move out to the edges of the city to premises which are much cheaper to rent and that he can better afford . . . Eventually, his poor service caused a decline in his business and started to eat into his profits.

Not fancy, but cheap

A successful chain of salvage shops has the slogan: 'We're not fancy, but we're cheap'. This chain has been successfully built up from a one-shop business. Each outlet is now packed with people picking up bargains by the basketful. The chain is open and honest about its no-frills business. The customers know this, and enjoy the bargain-basement, jumble-sale style of merchandising that the shops offer. There are no pretensions to being anything else. The shops are inexpensive, so the tills are ringing, business is booming and the sales volumes keep increasing!

Declare temporary limitations

Always be honest about the limitations of your business or any aspects of your services or products.

For example, when your chef cuts her hand and is taken off to hospital for stitches, let your customers know and ask how they wish to proceed, given the limitations under which you are now operating.

How many of us have waited over an hour for a meal at a restaurant, only to be told there is a delay? If we had known earlier, we could have chosen to pace our drinking, ordered pre-prepared food or left to go to another restaurant. More importantly, we would have respected the restaurant rather than telling our friends about the long delays. Bad word-of-mouth advertising is the most damaging advertising there is.

Only cold food

A group of my friends went to a birthday lunch at a local restaurant one day in winter. The owner met them at the door to say the gas stoves in the kitchen were not working. The customers' disappointment was quickly overcome when she told them the restaurant had some very special salad and cold dishes on the day's menu and would offer them each a free glass of good wine with their meals. As well, each would receive a token for another free glass of wine next time they visited the restaurant—when the stoves *were* working.

What a great save! The restaurateur had turned a disaster into a great marketing positive—just by being honest and backing that honesty up with incentives to encourage loyalty from her customers.

> My friends did stay. The service was better than usual,
> and they had positive stories to tell about the restaurant
> over the next few days and weeks with their individual
> good word-of-mouth advertising.

This story illustrates several important aspects of being honest with your customers:

- quick action with personal communication about the temporary limitations;
- seamless, relevant extra compensation for the customer;
- further incentives to encourage loyalty in the face of adversity; and
- turning each customer into an advocate when they could have been disappointed customers who never went there again—and told their friends not to either.

Communicating who is in charge

Your customers need to know who they should speak to about any issue. It is therefore important to provide information about who is in charge of any aspect of your business, including services, processes and product ranges. This may not always apply, but in trades and the service professions, it is important that customers are aware who has the power and authority to make key decisions about discounts or refunds.

Who's between your customer's wallet and your till?

My friend David's thirteen-year-old son, Jon, arranged with a local toy shop to purchase a specially priced army of toy soldiers for his birthday (approximately $300 worth). This was negotiated at length, and a record kept on the shop computer to match Jon's printout.

Jon and David organised to go night shopping and duly

presented the printout so that the special birthday present could be paid for and collected. The staff member informed them that he had only been working at the toy shop for five days and didn't know how to find the list on the computer. As well, he was alone in the shop and didn't have a phone number to call the owner or manager for help and advice on what to do.

He wouldn't fill the order or confirm a price because the shop owner had instructed him that he was not allowed to discount at all. This was despite the fact that the advertised shop policy was that when a customer bought a full army of toys there was a discount of 10 per cent.

The staff member clearly did not want to be bothered with this little kid (with $300 to spend!) and really wanted to get back to the war game he was playing with some other customers. So he told them to 'Come back tomorrow when the boss is here', leaving this boy crushed that his birthday gift was delayed.

His father, needless to say, would have preferred never to do business with that store again and had to restrain himself from giving his own brand of customer feedback and being an instant difficult customer.

This story illustrates a failure to use many of the rules of good customer service. Although the shop was clear about discount policy, because the people with authority were not in the shop at the time (and they hadn't adequately communicated the policy to the new staffer), Jon simply could not collect his toys. During one of the busiest trading sessions—Thursday night shopping—the manager had literally left his business crippled, unable to perform anything but the most straightforward service transactions.

The direct customer (Jon) was left disappointed—the best way to destroy loyalty. Jon's father was angry on behalf of his son because Jon had planned and looked forward to this moment—the collection of his much-prized toys.

Ideally, it should not be necessary to have a special person in charge because any staff members should have the authority, skills and knowledge to answer any question and fix any problem. But in most small businesses there is an owner or manager who has superior knowledge about the business's processes, products and services. This person usually also has the discretion to change standard policies or practices on the spot to better meet the expectations of customers with special or non-standard needs.

Because every business makes occasional mistakes, you need to make provision for customers to go to any person within your business with the power and authority to make decisions so they can put things right when they go wrong (see Chapter 8). Make sure such a person is always available, and that such decisions can be made quickly and with minimal fuss. Do not leave your staff stranded and your business crippled.

Overview

Being open and honest with your customers about any limitations or problems is about gaining their respect and loyalty so they become advocates for your business. It means making clear as soon as possible:

- what your services cost;
- how well you perform them; and
- who is in charge of every aspect of service transactions.

Your business practises openness and honesty for two reasons:

- Your customer is fully aware of what you *cannot* do for them and any alternatives you have in place to provide them with an excellent service transaction experience anyway.
- You provide the customer with an honest assessment, leading them to respect you. This builds loyalty, and

49

your customers will become valuable advertisers and advocates for your business.

Being open and honest: questions for your business

- Are you and your staff honest from the start if you know you cannot meet the expectations of your customers?
- Do you and your staff actively and promptly keep customers informed about any changes to service delivery?
- Do you and your staff ensure customers are informed about any unavoidable changes in service costs?
- Do you and your staff keep your customers informed about who is in charge of their service transaction?

Practical tips for being open and honest with your customers

- Each month, ask one customer whether they have been negatively surprised about any aspect of doing business with you. Then design a way to provide information to your customers to eliminate the chance of similar surprises for other customers.
- Make sure you display clear, simple signs or supply information brochures about your fees and charges.
- If customers tell you about things you haven't done well, be honest with other customers about it—and then work to improve.
- Ask your customer what 'bugs' them about doing business with you—then work out ways to fix the 'bugs'.

---

chapter 4

RULE 4: OFFER CHOICE TO YOUR CUSTOMERS

You can improve your customer service by offering customers a choice wherever possible.

It is important to give your customers the opportunity to choose how service is delivered. Offering several options indicates to customers that your business is flexible enough to cater for all their needs.

This good service rule is closely linked to *consulting your customers* (see Chapter 5) because by asking your customers about their preferences, you are more likely to meet their needs.

Several areas of the service transaction lend themselves to providing options for your customers. They are:

- costs, which may be discounted in certain circumstances;
- delivery methods and times; and
- product lines and varieties.

However, *too* much choice will only confuse customers. It can become too hard to make a choice at all. So, as with many of the other rules of good service, achieving a balance for the customer is important.

Payment options

Many businesses offer a variety of methods to pay for services and products. These can include cash, credit cards, electronic funds transfer (EFTPOS), cheques, monthly accounts and lay-by. These days, customers expect most or all of these options to be available. Ensure that you provide information to your customers about all payment methods used by your business.

> ### Flexibility in choice
> Recently, a friend of mine had some clothing alterations done. The invoice for the work, handed to her when she dropped off the garments, was stamped 'cash only'. She interpreted this to mean cash, EFTPOS or debit cards, but not cheques or credit cards. Much to her surprise, she found that 'cash only' meant just that. No other method of payment was available. This meant my friend had to travel several storeys down into the business district, find a cash point machine and draw money out of her account, then return to the business to pay for and collect her garments. She was very annoyed and vowed never to use that business again. As she spends several hundred dollars per year on alterations, this was a substantial business loss to that very small company, not to mention the cost to the business of her bad word-of-mouth advertising.

Problems such as this are linked to *effective communication* (see Chapter 1). The company had gone to the effort to communicate its restricted policy on payment but it was still unclear. Sometimes, in the interests of *being open and honest* about your business limitations (see Chapter 3), it is useful to tell your customers what you do *not* do. In this case, it would have been helpful to list forms of payment which were unacceptable.

More importantly, you should examine your business practices to see whether there is an area such as payment methods where you may be able to provide more options to your customers, and thus improve your service to

them.

Delivery methods and times

Flexibility is at the heart of offering choice to your customers, and this particularly applies to *times* for delivery of services.

Many service businesses, such as plumbers and electricians, offer a great home-based service. Other businesses deliver products to your home. However, as discussed in Chapter 1, many businesses do not offer a choice of delivery times, often causing major inconvenience to the customer. Even worse is an appointment that is not kept. Businesses argue that it is difficult to schedule home visits accurately. However, some companies *can* do it, which means it is possible if the correct processes are put in place.

It is important to develop good diary management skills to achieve this flexibility in service delivery for your customers. It is also good to offer some flexibility in the times that you will be available to deliver a service. See Chapter 1 for further information about diary management.

Providing options

It is a fact of modern life that many people work long hours and are simply not available to accept deliveries of services or products during normal working hours. You may therefore need to offer delivery outside of normal business hours. Maybe you can allocate one day of each week where you either start really early or work late to provide deliveries or services. My local dentist, for example, offers appointments outside of normal business hours. Take time off during a quieter part of the week to offset the extra hours.

Product range

No customer group is homogeneous—within every customer group there are different requirements. By providing a choice of product, you are catering to the element of personal choice.

It is not necessary to keep every possible variety of a product line in stock; however, take note if your customers regularly show interest in a particular product. If you don't stock the product, discuss it with the customer and weigh up the benefits of stocking that product. It may mean you will gain and keep a regular customer.

Customer behaviour: choice and limitations

If you want to observe how customers assert their choice in a business, just look at some of the big international burger and fast food chains. Their standardisation of services and products is the benchmark on which other businesses model their practices. Walk past any McDonald's and see the burger wrappings discarded with pieces of gherkin or other food material in them. That's because the service and products at McDonald's are completely standardised and the customer gets choice within a limited range only. They have to remove what they don't want from the standard format.

Your small business must offer choice if it is to survive. However, like McDonald's, the choice can be within a certain range of both service and products. If your business is based on a formula of limited, specialised products at very competitive prices, look to where else you can offer flexibility and choice for your customers. For instance, you may be able to offer choice to your customers through flexible payment and delivery options.

Flexibility is one of the great advantages that small business has over large conglomerates. In your small business, you are lean and trim and in touch with your customers. You can respond to their needs and be flexible in what you offer them. Exploit that difference!

Making assumptions

A computer technician took it upon himself to change a customer's Internet operating system to Netscape without asking because he thought it was a better system. He made the mistake of assuming that his personal preference would be the same as that of the customer and failed to consult with them on the issue.

This is a good example of the way many of the rules of good customer service overlap. In this case, the technician not only failed to give the customer a choice, but also failed to consult the customer.

Netscape turned out to be completely inappropriate for a paper communication-based small business that wanted emails delivered to their customers with letter presentation quality. Once the situation was explained, the technician understood why it was not OK for that particular customer to have Netscape on her system. But he wasted time and money by having to return at the customer's convenience to put the problem right.

Overview

Offering choice to your customers is about flexibility of delivery and options. By asking your customers what they prefer, and offering a range of options, they are better equipped to make a choice that suits their needs. Ensure that a full range of options is available to your customers at all times.

Offering choice to your customers: questions for your business
- Do you and your staff always provide options to your customers about how they will pay for and when they will receive your products or services?
- Do you provide a range of products and services for your customers?

Practical tips for offering choice to your customers
- Randomly ask two customers whether they believe you provide sufficient choice to them.

- Ask those customers where they would like your business services to be more flexible—then work out a way to achieve this. If you can't be more flexible, find a way to effectively communicate to your customer why this is not possible.
- Make a list of your service processes. Go through the list and make sure that you have the best standard method of delivering to your customers and an alternative for customers with different preferences, as well as when things go wrong.

chapter 5

RULE 5: CONSULT WITH YOUR CUSTOMERS

It is essential to keep in touch with what your customers think about your service so that you can evolve to better meet their needs. This means checking with your customers that you're on the right track from *their* perspective. Consulting with your customers means:

- having discussions with them;
- seeking advice and information from them; and
- taking the views they offer into consideration when you are making decisions about changing your service practices.

Asking your customers for feedback is a very important aspect of good service. At a very basic level, this means saying things like: '*How* may I help you?' It is also about asking the customer which service or level of product they would prefer.

This is another aspect of customer service where small business has an edge over big business. You can survey customers easily and inexpensively because you are so close to them. Big business has to pay huge amounts to survey customers because its managers and executives are so distant from them. In many cases, they don't trust their staff to ask the important questions. But surveys often fail to give information about the specific actions they need to take to improve service.

Your advantage is that you can ask simple questions like:

- What's the one thing you would like us to improve about our service to you to make it easier to be our customer?

- What's the one thing we do very badly from your perspective?
- What bugs you about doing business with us?
- What would you like us to do differently when we are serving you?

This is the most inexpensive way of consulting with your customers and it gives you *actionable input* (that is, information that you can act on to improve your service to your customers).

Customer feedback

Feelgood feedback

If all you want is feelgood feedback, ask your customers: 'What's the best thing that we do when we are serving you/doing business for you?' It'll be the good news that will make you feel good. But it won't help you improve your business. Feelgood feedback does have a minor role to play because it tells you what you are doing well which you should continue to do. However, you need to dig deeper.

My observation is that in businesses where only feelgood feedback is gathered, very little attention is paid to what needs to be done better or differently to improve the business or service transaction processes. To better manage the service transaction, you need to know what your customers think about your performance against the nine guiding rules of good service.

Measuring customer perceptions

When you seek customer feedback, you are attempting to discover how customers experience the service transaction with your business. If we again look at Figure I.1 from the introduction to this book, we are trying to understand what happens in the space between your business standards and your customers. It is your customers who can provide this vital information.

Figure 5.1 The Service Transaction

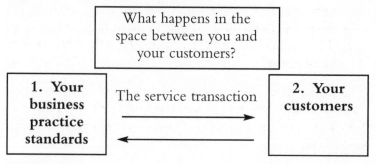

<table>
<tr><td></td><td colspan="2">What happens in the space between you and your customers?</td><td></td></tr>
<tr><td>1. Your business practice standards</td><td colspan="2">The service transaction →
←</td><td>2. Your customers</td></tr>
</table>

Knowledge is power

There's a very old-fashioned saying in customer service:

> If you are *happy* with our service, it's *nice* to know.
> If you are *unhappy* with our service, we *need* to know.

Although the idea may have been around for a long time, it is still a useful one. I recommend to my small business clients that they display a similar sign in the front service area of their business.

You need to know if your customers are unhappy with your service for many reasons:

- to alert you to problems in your business as soon as possible;
- so you can plan services and standards to meet the expectations of your customers;
- to avoid your customers feeling disappointed; and
- to avoid bad word-of-mouth advertising.

There is a very real possibility that your customers may be unhappy and may never use your business again. Without asking, you may not even know about it. The *attrition rate* refers to the gradual wearing away of your customer base, while *churn* means rapid turnover of customers. Both need to be avoided. If you are losing customers, you need to know why. Customer complaints and expressions of dissatisfaction are a good source of information, so encourage them.

Chapter 8, which looks at *putting things right when they go wrong*, provides more information on why you should encourage complaints and how it is ultimately beneficial for your business to receive them and manage them effectively and efficiently.

Actionable input

The main reason for asking customers what they think of your business is to gain *actionable input* from them. This means getting feedback from your customers so that you can take action to improve your business and service practices. Actionable input tells you what you need to *stop* doing, *continue* doing and *change* in your practices.

Questions to ask

There are three major questions you need to ask your customers:

- What do we do badly?
- What should we continue doing?
- What do we need to change?

What do we do badly?

If your customers think you do something badly, you need to take action to change this aspect of your business service. For example, a customer may say you need to stop playing really loud rock music in your shop because it is difficult to concentrate and to hear what you and your staff are saying. If you think music doesn't matter, think again—if it is sufficiently off-putting, it can cause a customer to walk away from your business.

Take care to listen to what the customer says. No matter

how unimportant it may seem to you, these are the things you need to consider changing.

Alternatively, a customer may say the staff don't pay attention to them, and they have to work too hard to ask questions about something they may want to purchase.

What should we continue doing?

The second question to ask your customers is: 'What should we continue doing?'—or 'What do we do well?' The response here will tell you why customers continue using your service even if they also believe you do some things badly. On one level, this feelgood feedback is important because it will reinforce positive aspects of your business, and can be passed on to your staff. However, as discussed above, be aware that feelgood feedback does not provide *actionable input* from your customers.

What do we need to change?

The third important question to ask your customers is 'What do we need to change?' This question is designed to find out what you need to do differently (though your responses need not be as urgent as to the first question on what you do badly).

Try this question with two loyal, long-term customers. Ask them outright: 'What do we need to change to make it easier for you to be our customer?' Then, once you feel safe enough, ask two *new* customers the same question. I guarantee that the answers will relate to the rules of good customer service covered in this book. Very rarely (if ever) will you get criticism about your technical capacity to competently perform the specialist work of your trade or profession—your business practice standards.

Make sure you ask these three questions on a regular basis. When busy, and when business is slow, ask the questions again and again. Record the responses and watch to see if there is a pattern to your quality of service during regular and noticeable cycles in your business and industry.

Most importantly, make the necessary changes to better meet your customers' expectations.

Customer satisfaction

Many companies, including large ones, believe they only need to know whether their customers are *satisfied* or whether the service the customers received was *satisfactory*.

However, recent research carried out by Dr Michael Edwardson, from the School of Marketing at the University of New South Wales, shows that what the customer uses to inform their decision-making about whether or not to use a business again are specific emotions such as happiness, humiliation and disappointment—not just their satisfaction rating. For instance, customer happiness is three times more related to intended loyalty than ratings of simple satisfaction. This shows why it is very important to know more than just a satisfaction rating from a customer. If you are serious about improving your service to build your customer base, and to differentiate your business from your competitors, the only question you really need to ask is 'What do you believe we need to do differently?'

Different methods of consultation

There are many conventional methods of consulting with customers (see Table 5.1). Some are relatively inexpensive, while others are more complex and more expensive to develop and implement.

Some methods are far better suited to the particular needs and circumstances of small businesses. My recommendation is that you use complaints information as part of your normal business practice, especially when making decisions on what should be done differently (see Chapter 8 on putting things right). On the other hand, specifically researching customer input does require actively seeking customers' views on issues to do with your business service practice.

Table 5.1: Methods of customer consultation

Method	Relative cost	Recommendation	Action
1 Complaints monitoring	$–$$	Yes, if you have good processes in place to capture the information. Gathers qualitative information. If managed really well, can also provide quantitative information.	Make sure all complaints are written against the rules of good service which have been broken. Check the list regularly and take action to ensure it doesn't happen again.
2 Suggestion schemes (staff and customers)	$–$$	Yes. Must be managed well and properly. Qualitative information only.	Have a box on the front counter with an easy, tear-off notepad. Offer a dinner for two each month as a prize for one randomly selected suggestion writer.
3 Consultation with other businesses	$–$$	Yes. A form of 'mystery shopping'. Best done with businesses in non-competitive areas. Good for picking up new ideas for doing things better and differently. Qualitative information only.	Join an industry group, attend their events and mix with the other attendees. Ask questions to learn about ideas to apply to your business.
4 Service surveys	$$–$$$	Yes. Recommended if done simply, inexpensively and well.	See the sample customer feedback form in the Appendix.

5 Focus groups	$$–$$$	Can be useful. Difficult to organise but good relationship-building opportunity.	Call four to six of your regular customers in for morning tea or a drink after work. Ask them the three key consultation questions and list their responses.
6 Customer panels	$$–$$$	Better for big business. Give quick feedback and can assist in gaining continuous feedback.	Conduct a regular monthly or quarterly meeting with your focus group.
7 Open days/ roadshows	$$–$$$	Better suited to big business.	Avoid. You are in small business, you don't have the time.
8 Opinion surveys	$$$–$$$	No. Expensive. Must be well designed and provide actionable input.	Avoid.

There are three ways of doing this:

- simply asking them face-to-face;
- having questionnaires or simple forms to complete; or
- developing and conducting comprehensive surveys.

Face-to-face customer research

Face-to-face questioning of your customers is the easiest and cheapest way to gain customer feedback. You already have yourself and your staff in the frontline, speaking with your customers and well-placed to ask the three simple questions listed above. However, consultation must be *regular* and *systematic*.

Another very easy way to gain simple actionable input from your customers is to ask: 'What bugs you about doing business with us?' Compile a list of the customers' 'bugs', then talk to your staff about ideas on how to fix the 'bugs'.

A very similar set of questions can be:

- What are we doing which you want us to stop doing?
- What are we doing which you want us to continue to do?
- What are we doing which you think we need to change?

These are really variations on the same theme, which have the potential to provide you with very valuable and potent ways to improve your business in the eyes of your customers.

Customer surveys

Copying other surveys

Many small businesses with limited resources simply copy ideas from surveys they have received. This is dangerous because so many are poorly designed. It is better to design your own survey to meet your specific information needs. To make it easy for you to design a good survey to get actionable input from your customers, a sample is provided in the Appendix to this book. I recommend you follow these guidelines when you develop your survey.

What to avoid

As customers, we encounter many different styles of customer feedback forms. Many are poorly designed from my perspective and only seek to gain satisfaction ratings or feelgood feedback. Figure 5.2 is an example of an ineffective form.

Figure 5.2: Poor feedback form (a)

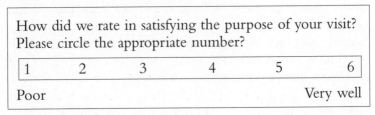

How did we rate in satisfying the purpose of your visit? Please circle the appropriate number?

1	2	3	4	5	6
Poor					Very well

No action can be taken in your business as the result of any of the possible responses to this question. All you have is information from a customer about how they 'rate' you. The responses don't provide any specific information to use in changing or improving your business processes.

Some surveys ask customers how they 'felt' about the service. 'Quality' is a term that is a bit like 'satisfaction'. It has many meanings and understanding of its meaning varies from person to person and from culture to culture. This means the question will provide you with responses that have no real, objective meaning. There is no actionable input as this sample shows:

Figure 5.3: Poor feedback form (b)

How did you feel about the quality of the service we provided you? Please circle the appropriate face.

As with the first sample, the question is, *what action can you take to improve your business from any of the possible responses to this question?*

Using simple faces such as the ones above helps businesses to simplify the surveying process. Some market research companies recommend this method if your customers base represents many different languages.

Take care when you are working to put together a customer survey to gain feedback from your customers. I am often called into companies to look at their survey results because they just don't know what to do with them. This is because the information does not meet the needs of the business: there is no good information on which to base the next decision-making step. Poor survey design is invariably the root cause of the problem. It means the business collects a whole lot of information about 'satisfaction' that cannot be used for decision-making. I usually advise clients to start again with a simpler, less expensive and more useful approach.

The remainder of this chapter examines some inexpensive, easy and useful ideas for consulting with customers to ascertain their expectations of your business.

What *not* to ask

Many companies confuse their *business* standards and processes with their *service transaction* processes. This chapter is about consulting with your customers to find out what they think you need to do differently to *serve* them better. Table 5.2 lists several questions you should avoid asking, and explains why.

Table 5.2: Questions to avoid

Question	Reason not to use
Was the service beyond your expectations, did it meet your expectations or was it below your expectations.	This question is too general. Service is made up of nine indicators. You need to measure each (or those which are most important to your business).

How was our product range?	What can the customer answer? The question is too general. And no answer will tell you *what* you need to do differently about your range of products.
How was the store environment?	This question is too general and does not measure a service indicator. The question forces the customer to give a qualified response about the environment. But what does this mean?
Did we treat you well?	What can the customer answer? The question is too general. And no answer will tell you *what* you need to do differently about the way you treat your customers.

Developing useable questionnaires

Moving up from simple questions such as 'What bugs you about doing business with us?', the next step is to design and administer simple questionnaires to some of your customers. Never try to survey all your customers unless you are a micro business with a few core, regular customers who are easy to contact and maintain a relationship with.

Measuring and counting service indicators

There are two types of information you can gather from your customers when you consult with them: qualitative and quantitative.

Quantitative information can be measured and counted. It is about the *quantity* or *number* of responses. This information converts well into tables and graphs to provide a snapshot of what the customer thinks.

Qualitative information is less easily quantified but makes *judgements* about our service provision. This information will vary from customer to customer and represents their *perceptions*. Usually the information comes from open-ended questions such as 'What do you think?'

A good survey gathers as much qualitative data as possible and then also gathers other quantitative information in the form of comments from the customer.

Measuring quality in service

We know that quality in service has three aspects:

- *conformance* to customer expectations;
- *cost* in terms of value for money; and
- *consistency*, or the same service or product standard every time.

Each of these is measurable and the answers to questions such as those below can be used to decide which areas of the service transaction and your business practice you need to improve. Remember the questions below provide only a basic foundation. A more comprehensive sample question-naire which incorporates and measures all these three aspects can be found in the Appendix.

In designing a simple three-question questionnaire to measure these three facets of service quality, you might ask the following:

Measuring conformance to customer expectations

1a. The service you received from us met your expectations:

Always   Mostly   Sometimes   Rarely   Never   Don't know

☐   ☐   ☐   ☐   ☐   ☐

1b. In what way did our service not meet your expectations?

Comment: Your business did not _____

_____

(*Note:* Any response other than 'Always' alerts you that you may need to ask other questions to find out which parts of your service delivery do not meet the expectations of customers.)

Measuring value for money

2a. You believe you received service that represented value for the money you paid our company:

Always Mostly Sometimes Rarely Never Don't know

☐   ☐   ☐   ☐   ☐   ☐

2b. In what way did our service represent poor value for your money?

Comment: The service (or product) was not good value for money because _____

_____

Measuring consistency in service

3a. The service you received was consistently good?

Always Mostly Sometimes Rarely Never Don't know

☐   ☐   ☐   ☐   ☐   ☐

3b. In what way was our service not consistent?

Comment: _____

_____

Developing and conducting your own comprehensive surveys

If your business is big enough to warrant it, simple surveys and questionnaires are one way of consulting with your customers and gaining actionable input. Take great care about what you ask in your surveys. If it is handled well, a survey does not have to be expensive to administer. You can break the process into manageable parts. Remember, there are a lot of fairly useless surveys in the marketplace which are simply designed to gain feelgood feedback and satisfaction ratings from customers. Your business is too important to risk conducting that sort of consultation with your customers. Don't just copy surveys because they look OK to you. *You need to know what you need to do better and you need to know as quickly as possible.* When you have completed a survey of your customers' views it is important to implement the changes with the minimum of disruption to your customers.

Measuring business versus service standards

The other main style of survey is that which asks your customers about your business practice standards. Many businesses ask about *product* rather than *service* transactions. But we are concerned about exploring the service transaction—that space between your business and your customer.

The nine guiding rules of good service provide you with the topics that need to be measured when it comes to the service transaction. You will notice that there is nothing in the rules about how hot the food is, or the appearance of your shop, or the colour of the product. That's because those things are about your *business* standards, not about *service*.

When designing your own survey, make sure it is the *service* that you measure—not anything else. The key measure for service is consistency. For this reason, consistency is the criterion against which each of the rules in this book should be measured. The questions need to be phrased as statements of outcome, which are then measured against a Likert scale of consistency indicators. (The Likert scale is a method of measuring the views of a survey participant across a meaningful range of possible responses, designed by Renesis Likert in 1932.) In other words, the questions are designed to find out how often the customer experienced good performance in terms of the nine rules of good service.

The sample questions in the Appendix measure each of the nine rules of good service against the criterion of *consistency*. You need to know how consistent you are for several reasons:

- The customer may have come to expect a high standard from you and will be disappointed if they do not receive it all the time.
- You need to be able to identify whether there is something that is regularly or intermittently going wrong with your service and business processes.

Building your own survey

The sample survey in the Appendix measures each of the nine guiding rules for good customer service. You can alter the questions to match your needs or you can select just some of them to test with your customers. As you work through these sample questions, see how:

- they reflect the nine guiding rules of good customer service;
- each can be measured;
- you can adapt the questions to meet your needs;
- you can take just one set of questions about one aspect of the service transaction and see what your customers think.

You may like to take one rule a month and consult with your customers about their perceptions of your performance
on that indicator of good customer service. Just remember to

always measure your consistency in meeting the nine guiding rules of good customer service.

Each question in the Appendix deals with some aspect of each of the nine guiding rules of good service. You can change this survey to meet your needs and to best reflect what is most important for *your* business. The important thing is to stick to the nine rules to guide your thinking.

Once you have started to consult with your customers using some of these questions, it may become obvious that some things are more important to your customers than others. *Concentrate on the questions that will get you actionable input on those issues from your customers.*

Overview

You need to keep in touch with what your customers think about your service so you can change and adapt your service processes to better meet their needs.

Checking with your customers that you are on the right track from *their* perspective is the driving concept behind this rule of good service.

Asking your customers for their feedback is one of the most important aspects of good service. At a very basic level, this rule is about asking things like: 'What should we do differently to better serve you?' It is also about asking the customer which service or level of product they would prefer you to offer.

Consulting with your customers: questions for your business

- Do you and your staff ask customers about their preference for product selection?
- Do you and your staff ask your customers about their preference for service delivery and speed?
- Do you ask your customers for their opinion about your services?

Practical tips for consulting with your customers
- Ask three customers what they think:
  - your business does badly;
  - your business does well;
  - your business should do differently.
- Ask two customers per week: 'What is the one thing we need to improve about the way we do business with you?' Use the customers' answers to guide your decisions on making changes to your service processes.
- Before you make any changes to your service processes, ask three customers what they think of your proposals.

chapter 6

RULE 6: BE COURTEOUS TO YOUR CUSTOMERS

Courtesy towards customers is such an obvious part of good customer service that it can actually be overlooked. So often, we experience indifference or rudeness as customers.

Being courteous to your customers is simply about demonstrating the best of good manners to your customers at all times. Every customer should be treated the way you would a very important stranger. Being courteous is the main ingredient for building a positive relationship with a customer so that you become their provider of choice in your business area.

There are two main indicators of this good service rule. The first is that employees of your business (who should *always* wear name badges) offer courteous service to your customers at all times. This good service rule is about greeting your customers in a manner appropriate to the time of the day. It is also about maintaining appropriate levels of eye contact and distance between you and the customer. As well, staff need to make the customer feel at ease in your business so that they experience pleasant emotions and will be more likely to return.

This good service rule is often referred to as the 'smiles and hellos' of customer service. Many businesses (including large ones) make the mistake of assuming that this behaviour is all there is to good customer service. As this book shows, there is far more involved. But courtesy is important because it represents the compulsory first steps in the service transaction.

The second indicator that you are being appropriately courteous to your customers is that you make services available equally to your customers if they are entitled to them and those services are clearly operated to suit *their* convenience.

Offering courteous service to your customers

Courtesy is about good, old-fashioned manners. It includes:

- acknowledging your customers as soon as they enter your business in an appropriate manner;
- identifying yourself to your customers;
- identifying other staff if relevant;
- treating customers with respect at all times;
- using customers' preferred names where you can, and remembering them;
- using the customer's preferred title (e.g. Mr, Mrs, Ms, Dr); and
- remembering aspects of their preferences about doing business with you.

Acknowledging your customers as soon as they enter your business

Acknowledging a customer is the very first step in customer service. It is the beginning of the service transaction and can set the mood for how your customers will view you, your staff and your business. You may have spent a great deal of money setting up your business, yet in these precious few introductory moments you can effectively waste all the time, money and effort so far expended on the business simply by failing to acknowledge your customers in an appropriate way.

When a customer enters your business, make it clear you know that they are there. This must be done even if you are really busy and there are people queued up at the counter or in the reception area. Simply saying 'Good afternoon' or 'Good morning' is the best way to do this. However, just making eye contact is sufficient if you are very busy. It says to the customer: 'You are important and I know you are there'. It is even better to say: 'I'll be with you in a moment'. Customers are not stupid. They can see that you are busy and they will appreciate your acknowledgment.

How many times have you heard your friends complain about how they went into a business where the staff were chatting 'about the weekend' and not paying any attention to the customers. Ensure this never happens in your business.

Pie in the eye

A friend recently went to buy a pie in a specialist pie shop. When he entered, neither of the two staff at the counter looked at him, although they must have known he was there.

The shop was a new retail concept which only sold savoury and sweet pies, and had standardised systems and processes for selling the product. My friend wanted to know how it all worked and, being a health-conscious vegetarian, wanted to ask some questions about the product to help him decide. But although he was the only customer, he could not make eye contact with either of the staff—they were too busy doing the more important work of wiping down benches and tidying up the counter. Eventually he had to ask: 'Will you please help me?'

This is not only bad manners on behalf of the staff, it is bad business—and bad *for* business. The acknowledgment of a customer is like welcoming someone into your home. Would you ignore a guest who had just arrived? Of course not. Yet every day in our shops and businesses, customers like my friend are having to ask for help rather than being asked whether the business can help *them*.

Customers are special guests with whom you need to build a relationship. They are the guests who will hand over their hard-earned money so that you can run your business, pay yourself and your staff and feed yourself and your family. Treat them as if they are that special—because they are! Acknowledge them when they arrive before you do anything else.

Identifying yourself to your customers

Building a relationship with your customers involves using their name where possible and letting them know your name so they can use it if they choose. If you are dealing with your customers face-to-face, name badges are the best way to do this.

The name badge should be worn on either the left or right hand side of the chest in the lapel position and should clearly display at least your first name. The lettering should be in bold and about a centimetre high, and should be a clear dark colour on a light background.

Keep the information on the name badge simple:

- names—given (compulsory) and family (optional);
- company name; and
- company logo.

Where staff wear their name badges is important. It can have a direct impact on the confidence customers feel in interacting with your staff. I went to a conference once that was attended predominantly by males from the engineering professions. The name badges fitted all the criteria for being serviceable (large, bold, dark lettering), but they were on long chains worn around the neck. This caused the actual name plate to hang just below waistline on the many men (and few women) who were present. As a female in the minority, I did not learn many names. In such a setting, I just could not contemplate peering down to the below-the-belt regions of all the men I was being introduced to. When I shared my discomfort with some of the men, they agreed that for them it was equally embarrassing and difficult.

Because it is so important to be able to read name tags, make sure they are properly positioned, fastened and straight.

Don't forget to wear a name badge yourself—even if you are the managing director or the owner of your business. It is even more important for customers to know you and remember your name.

Who, me?

This is a big business story, but the message is important for any business. It concerns a large business where some 3500 staff were employed. It was undergoing a huge restructure with lay-offs and a great deal of organisational turbulence. The chief executive officer conducted regular briefing sessions for staff to inform them of the latest developments. His executive team would join him on the stage of the training theatre and deliver brief statements on what was going on and what was planned for their divisions. At the end of each meeting, the CEO would ask: 'Are there any questions?'

One day, one brave soul raised her hand and said: 'Yes. I'm new here. So who are you all up there?'

Not one of the executive team had introduced themselves or explained their roles. The whole executive team, from the top down, had made the mistake of assuming that they were so important that everyone would just know who they were—despite the fact that it was such a huge organisation. It is easy to be mistaken about our own importance in the eyes of others.

Take a little time out to contemplate the following questions.

- Have you ever forgotten the name of someone you have just been introduced to?
- Have you ever forgotten the name of someone important—even if only momentarily?
- Have you ever forgotten the name of someone really close to you?

If you are like most of the participants in my training sessions, you would have answered 'Yes' to at least one of those questions. That is why wearing name badges during any service transaction is so vital. Like us, customers easily forget names. It is your responsibility to work to help the customer—not the other way around.

Identifying other staff if relevant

If you need to refer a customer to anyone else in your business, always use the other staff member's name and position. For example, say: 'Mary from the accounts department will help you with your questions'. You must do the same if you are transferring a customer's telephone call to another staff member. Tell the caller, for example: 'I will just transfer you to Bob in the Deliveries section and he will be able to help you'.

Never just send a customer off to another section of the business without any introduction. Equally, never just point to a staff member and refer to them as 'that one over there'. It is bad manners to do so and shows a lack of respect for your fellow staffers.

Treating customers with respect at all times

Dining at a restaurant, my friend Jan ordered a small serve of pasta for herself and a regular serve for her partner Bob. When the meals came, Jan thought that hers seemed a generous serve so she checked with the waitress that it was definitely the small serve. The waitress confirmed this. But on settling the bill, Jan noticed that they had been charged for a large serve. The cost wasn't that much more but on principle she did not want to pay for something she had not ordered. When she queried this with the manager/cashier, he at first treated Jan as if she were lying. Then, after Jan insisted that she had made her order clear and checked it on delivery, he asked in a loud and aggressive manner: 'Well, did you eat it all?' By this time, others were queued up to pay and could overhear the conversation. After pausing to recover from shock, Jan replied that his question was not relevant. The manager begrudgingly altered the bill. My friends left feeling angry and embarrassed and vowed never to return.

Several rules were broken here:

- First, the waitress was unhelpful because she did not listen carefully to the order. This is where the errors started to occur.
- Second, there was no attempt to fix things when they went wrong and the customer was treated like a criminal or a liar when she pointed out the error.
- Finally, the manager was very discourteous in his handling of the situation.

If any of your staff (or you!) treat your customers in such a manner, immediately remove them from contact with your customers because they are doing irreparable damage to your business.

In this example, for the price of a few extra grams of pasta, the manager did an enormous amount of damage to his business, which possibly cost him thousands of dollars in bad word-of-mouth advertising.

Using customers' names

Our given names are very special to us as individuals, so we appreciate it when people take the time and make the effort to remember and use our preferred names during conversation.

When businesses take the time to learn their customers' names and the staff both remember and use them, it makes customers feel important, welcome and remembered. They feel your business cares about them.

This adds to the positive feelings we want our customers to experience so they will return to do further business with us—and, more importantly, tell others about us in good word-of-mouth advertising.

There are some simple ways to learn a customer's name. A freshly made fruit juice stall uses a system of asking customers their given name to place them in a queue, rather than issuing numbers. They write the customer's name on the order and, when it is ready, the staff who have prepared it call out the name. 'Two mango specials for Stephanie!' is a much better and far more courteous way to treat a customer than calling out 'Number 43!'

As well, names can be gleaned from credit and debit cards when customers hand them to you (although it is better to find out a name at the beginning of the transaction). Alternatively, just ask 'What is your name please?' or 'May I use your name, please?' Never be embarrassed to ask a customer to repeat the name, spell it or write it down for you if you miss it the first time. The customer will appreciate the effort you take to get it right.

On the opposite side of the coin, *never* use inappropriate terms of endearment with your customers. These include cutesie names such as Honey, Love, Lovey, Dear, Dearie, Mate and many others that I am sure you have heard. In business, it is inappropriate to deal with your customers in such a manner and you do so at the risk of irritating or angering them.

Nor should you abbreviate their names. An example of this is when your customer says his name is Jonathon, and you immediately call him Jon. The rule here is to copy whatever the customer calls himself or herself unless they instruct or guide you otherwise. Thus, a Jennifer is a Jennifer—not Jenny, Jens or Jen. Even if you like to shorten names because you think it makes your service delivery friendlier, don't do it.

Using correct titles

Some people don't care about titles and others do. It is best to check with the customer about their preference when using titles such as Mr, Mrs, Miss, Ms, Dr or Professor. As with any good customer service practice, avoid guessing where possible.

I recently had a business meeting with a senior, plain-clothes police officer at a coffee shop to discuss some issues of organisational culture. The attendant at the table called my business acquaintance 'Sir' throughout our meeting. However, she repeatedly addressed me as 'young lady'.

This is not an appropriate manner in which to address customers. If the table attendant had correctly used parallel language for my acquaintance and me she would have called him 'Sir' and me 'Madam' or 'Ma'am'. If she had done the reverse she should have called me 'young lady' and he 'young gentleman'!

A good test of the appropriateness of the language you are using to address your customers is to apply it to other customer segments. For her to call my business acquaintance 'young gentleman' would have seemed ridiculous. It was also unprofessional for her to address me as she did.

Staff in small businesses also need to be aware of cultural factors when it comes to dealing with customers. Some cultures are much more formal and find it offensive for first or given names to be used in a service context. Others don't care. Set a high standard that matches your business, ensure your standard will not be offensive to any of your customers and deliver the titles and greetings accordingly. Ask the customer how they prefer to be addressed, rather than guessing.

Remembering aspects of customers' preferences

Customers love to be treated as 'regulars' by businesses. This means the business remembers the customer's product and service delivery preferences. This aspect of good customer service is connected to *providing a single point of contact* for the customer (see Chapter 1).

Hotels have perfected this practice of remembering specific customer preferences. Many use sophisticated computer tracking systems to help them remember what customers like. In a small business, a small index card system can be just as effective. If you know John Jones is always in a hurry and likes fast service, note it on his card. That way, any staffer who serves Mr Jones can provide appropriate service—or explain at the outset why this won't be possible (see Chapter 3, on *being open and honest* with customers).

Any quirky behaviours which set a particular customer apart in your mind can provide hints about how they like to do business with you. Tailor your service accordingly and you will build a strong relationship with the customer.

Offering service to meet the customer's convenience

You are in business to serve customers in order to earn a living. So focus on providing products or services in a manner that is convenient for your customers. A small Internet service provider employed technical staff from 9.00 a.m. until 6.00 p.m. Customers often complained that when they rang for help at night, the technical people did not respond until the next morning, when they were at work. The busiest time for calls for help from customers was between 8.30 p.m. and midnight each night, but the owner refused to pay penalty rates to have technicians on call after hours. Clearly, the business wasn't meeting the convenience of the customers. This business had an 80 per cent churn rate at the time, which meant that 80 per cent of its customers were leaving every month. The owner was therefore forced into a cycle of desperately advertising to attract new customers—only to lose 80 per cent of them every month.

Eventually, a larger company that had 'after-hours' technical help bought him out, calmed the churn rate down and continued to boom based on a policy of service at the customer's convenience.

The same applies to deliveries. Make every effort to deliver at a time that suits your customer.

Overview

The importance of being courteous towards any customer or potential customer cannot be overstated. It is simply about good manners and making an effort.

Use appropriate greetings, maintain appropriate levels of eye contact and distance, and make the customer feel at ease in your business so that they experience pleasant emotions and will be more likely to return. Employees should wear name badges, and services should be available to all customers at a time that suits *them*. Finally, remember and use customers' names and appropriate titles, and make them feel like 'regulars' by remembering their preferences and using this information to provide better service.

Being courteous to your customers: questions for your business

- Do you and your staff always wear name badges when on duty?
- Do you and your staff always identify yourselves and the name of your business when answering the telephone?
- Do you and your staff always acknowledge each and every customer as soon as they enter your building/shop/office?
- Are you and your staff always polite and well-mannered to your customers and to each other when in front of the customers?
- Do you and your staff always thank your customers if they point out any aspect of your service which has not met their expectations?
- Do you and your staff always thank your customers when they raise a specific complaint with you?

Practical tips for being courteous to your customers
- Within three seconds, make sure you and your staff acknowledge, by eye contact, every customer who enters your business.
- Have well-designed, attractive name badges for staff to wear while on duty in your business.
- Wear a name badge yourself at all times while on duty in your business.
- Find a way to ask customers their name in the first minute of the interaction, then use their name for the rest of the service transaction.
- Ask two customers a week whether they find the staff appropriately courteous at all times.

chapter 7

RULE 7: BE HELPFUL TO YOUR CUSTOMERS

Being helpful to your customers enhances the service transaction experience for them, and builds loyalty to your business.

Being helpful is different from being courteous. It relates to *assisting* the customer, whereas courtesy is about being polite.

Helpful employees work to meet customers' needs by providing the best possible service to all customers, at the convenience of those customers.

Being helpful to your customers is about developing a 'can do' attitude for them. It means helping the customer to achieve or purchase what they want, even if you can't supply it immediately. It is finding a way to do what the customer wants, or referring them to another business that can.

A friend's daughter's wedding was to be a formal morning tea for 120 people in a vast parkland by the river. The family was very concerned that the celebration be held in the right spot, making best use of the sunshine and shade for the time of the day. Some weeks before the wedding, the owner of the business met the mother of the bride at the park and went out of his way to establish exactly what it was she wanted so that he could pass it on to his staff and make sure her needs were met. This made my friend feel very important, as if what she wanted was achievable and no trouble at all.

Meeting customers' needs requires good listening and observation skills. If a customer is rushing, don't start chatting about the weather. This is the time to say: 'I see you are in a hurry, Sir/Madam. Is there anything I can do to help you?' This gives them the opportunity to clearly state their needs so you can assist them in the shortest possible time.

Sometimes I go into a store and stand there at the service counter, timing staff to see how long it takes them to notice they have a customer. Or I count how many customers are not being served while staff are standing around chatting. When they finally do respond to my presence, often staff just say 'Hello' or 'Good day' and nothing else. They expect the customer to tell them what they require without offering to be helpful (so far, they have only been courteous).

I enjoy replying 'Hello' (with a smile, of course) and just continue standing there. There's always a moment of confusion, which is usually followed with 'Is someone helping you?' to which I reply the obvious: 'No'. Only then do the staff ask me what I require, or inquire how they might help me. Try this someday to show clearly the difference between courtesy and helpfulness.

Make sure you and your staff always link courtesy and helpfulness and that they (and you) understand the difference—because your customers certainly do!

Many big businesses with large call centres provide very effective training in courtesy. However, the systems and processes used, which require them to operate from standardised scripts, prevent them being helpful. When call centre staff are not helpful and the customer is giving them a serve of phone rage, they often react with the most amazingly courteous statements. This often infuriates the callers because it feels like they are banging their heads against a brick wall—they just don't receive the response they need. It is a perfect system to create a 'difficult' customer.

We are not here to be helpful!

I often buy food from an exclusive, well-publicised organic food shop. It has a pleasant atmosphere, with lots of signs urging all its customers to take good care of the environment. It offers paper bags rather than plastic, encourages customers to have purchases packed into recycled boxes and generally demonstrates very environmentally sound policies and practices. Attached to the food and produce section of the shop is a café that is owned by the same people. Generally, the café has very strict and inflexible rules about what size containers food can be purchased in (all plastic!) and what can be mixed with what.

One day, I watched a woman trying to buy her take-away lunch. She wanted a substantial rice patty (about 6 cm in diameter) with some salad. The policy of the shop was to serve the patty in a medium-sized, round, plastic takeaway container. The salads were served in a variety of oblong plastic containers and were costed accordingly. The two were served in separate containers and this was not negotiable. The customer wanted her small serve of salad and the patty to be placed in the same large oblong container, but was told this was not possible.

The customer had wanted to save on packaging and have the measured, standardised amounts of food (for which she was prepared to pay the set prices) put into the same large container. But the young counter attendant had been well trained in the rules of the shop and kept refusing any possible solution offered by the customer.

The customer pointed out how incongruous this practice was with the advertised policies and other practices of the shop. So the café manager was duly called out to arbitrate on the issue. And he stood by his staff member against the customer's wishes! She had to take the food in the two designated containers—despite offering to pay for a larger container and tip the food into it herself.

This is a classic illustration of rigid policies and practices being unhelpful. The staff were very courteous—and completely unhelpful. The shop was not displaying a *can do* attitude for the customer.

Let's examine what was happening in this service trans-action. There may have been very good reasons for the café's policies and rules. However, in operation they proved to be inflexible and irritating, as well as totally incongruous with the brand that the shop was obviously attempting to present. The customers of this business are driven by a strong environmentally oriented philosophy. The café's policy was in direct conflict with this philosophy, as well as forcing staff to be unhelpful to the customer.

Often the policies and rules of your business service actually prevent you from being helpful. Check your policies and practices to ensure that they match what you want people to think about your business. If a customer challenges them in any way and you are unwilling to be flexible and realistic, you have set both yourself and your staff up to be unhelpful to the customer.

Buy best, buy local

A friend's father lives in the country. He is setting up for his retirement there, so is in a position to purchase local services and products. Although he often travels to the city, he tries very hard to support local business as a way of building relationships with the community that he has chosen to live in—even though it costs more. He told me the story of how hard he had to work to purchase a roll of fencing wire.

He had priced the roll of wire at his large regional town and at the local hardware shop. The difference was only minor so he ordered locally. He was told the delivery day would be Thursday as the item was not in stock.

Come Thursday, he was informed that the proprietor had not ordered in time and the late order would have incurred a $30 surcharge, so it had been moved to the next Thursday without informing the customer or offering any form of apology.

The second Thursday arrived and there was still no wire. Apparently this was because there were no other orders to go with the wire, so the delivery was not made. This point was not explained to my friend's father at the beginning of the service transaction. The proprietor assured him that all was in order for a late delivery. He paid in advance to reinforce his need for the product, but the proprietor of the business offered neither apology for the delay nor thanks for the cheque.

This story illustrates how many of the nine rules of service can be present in any service transaction—especially when they are being broken.

- First, this is a story about how *unhelpful* a small business was in its service transaction. As well, we see the following rules being broken.
- The service was not *prompt*.
- No explanation was offered when *things went wrong*.
- The business was not *open and honest* about the delays in service or about special requirements for meeting an order (order in by set day of the week, number of orders required before delivery would occur).
- *Communication* was inadequate.
- *Choice* was not offered about delivery being at the customer's convenience.
- The owner was *discourteous* and said neither 'sorry' nor 'thank you' to the customer.
- Things were not *put right for the customer* when they went wrong.

None of this may have been so bad from the customer's viewpoint if the service had been both *helpful* and *courteous*. But it was not.

Overview

Being helpful to your customers differs from being courteous, but both aspects of customer service are equally important. Being helpful means finding a way to give the customer the product or service they require. It is a 'can do' approach to customer service.

Sometimes being helpful means being flexible in your business's policies and practices, and even referring the customer to another business if you are unable to help them.

Being helpful to your customers: questions for your business

- Do you and your staff work to help customers understand your service processes?
- Do you and your staff explain to customers how you can help in other ways if a customer's first preference is not possible?
- Do you and your staff do extra things to help customers find or access what they need?
- Do you and your staff offer extra services that are not part of the normal practice of your business?

Practical tips for being helpful to your customers
- With your staff, decide on three extra things a month that can be done to better help your customers get what they want.
- Offer a reward to the staff member who is most helpful, and who 'goes the extra mile' each week. Take nominations from your customers.
- Ask customers to tell you about anything you do which is inflexible and unhelpful—and change it!
- Notice when a customer is struggling in some way and offer to assist—for example, by offering to carry parcels to their car.

---

chapter 8

RULE 8: PUT THINGS RIGHT FOR YOUR CUSTOMERS

Things can go wrong in every service transaction. So managing complaints and putting things right for your customers as quickly as possible and with the minimum of fuss are important elements of good customer service.

This means managing complaints *effectively* by resolving them to the satisfaction of your customer—without damaging your business. The potential damage that can be done to your business comes from the bad word-of-mouth advertising spread by a customer if they are not satisfied with the way you manage their complaint. As well, if you don't resolve the issue quickly and effectively, considerable labour costs can result.

There are two main elements to managing customer complaints well:

- When things go wrong, your customers are offered an apology, a full explanation and a swift and effective remedy.
- Your business has well-publicised and easy-to-use complaints processes in place.

Let's take another look at Figure I.1 from the Introduction (see Figure 8.1). So far, this book has explained some of the guiding rules of good service practice. This chapter is about what to do *when that service transaction goes wrong*.

Defining a complaint

First, what is a complaint? The definition I prefer is that *a complaint is an expression of dissatisfaction that requires a response.*

Figure 8.1: Dealing with complaints

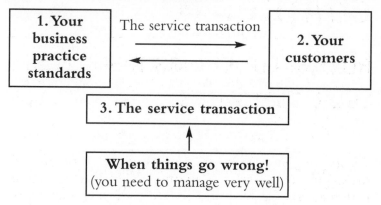

This means that, when things do go wrong, you accept it and move to fix the mistake or error as quickly as possible whle explaining to the customer how the mistake happened.

One participant in one of my public seminars asked me what he should have done when a young, very harried woman shouted at him 'You all make me sick!' and stormed out of the building. This isn't a complaint according to our definition, because there is no possibility of a response. There may have been a missed opportunity earlier in the service transaction, but the woman's outburst in itself does not constitute a complaint.

What do customers want?

We know customers want various experiences from the service transaction. As discussed in Chapter 1, first and most importantly, customers want a relationship. So it makes sense that, if a customer complains, it is because we failed to build or maintain a relationship with them or do the other things they wanted from our business (see Chapter 1).

If a customer complains, you should ask the following questions as they relate to the complaint:

- Was there anything we could have done differently to maintain a good relationship with that customer?

- Why didn't we get it right the first time?
- How come we were not accessible to our customers when they needed us to be?
- Why weren't we responsive to our customers?
- What do we need to do differently to make sure that we have knowledgeable people serving our customers?
- Why weren't we prompt in responding to our customers?
- Why didn't we keep our customers informed about processes and what they could have expected from us?
- Why didn't we provide follow up on any aspect of our product or service that we needed to?
- How and why did we provide unpleasant surprises to our customers?

Customers from hell

This chapter is concerned with managing complaints about service and business processes when they go wrong. There are, however, some customers who are particularly difficult. Chapter 10, 'Dealing with difficult customers', looks at the very small minority of customers who can never be understood nor satisfied, no matter what you do.

Encouraging complaints

So why should we encourage complaints? Research from both Australia and the United States shows that if we manage complaints well, it has a very positive effect on our customers' perceptions of our business. Dealing with a complaint quickly and to the satisfaction of the customer gives a 95 per cent-plus probability that they will return to do business with your company. On the other hand, if they are unhappy with the service and they don't let you know, the chance of them returning to do business with you drops to less than 40 per cent. In small business, you cannot afford to have this happen simply because customers find it hard to let you know where your processes have gone wrong and mistakes have been made.

Research by the Society of Consumer Affairs Professionals (SOCAP) in Australia reveals that dissatisfied customers:

- are more common than we think;
- would rather walk away from your business than fight with you; and
- tell others of their bad experience with you (more bad word-of-mouth advertising).

It is estimated that around 75–95 per cent of unhappy customers never contact management about their dissatisfaction. This is worrying data if it relates in any way to your business. If you examine the above points, there is something you can do about each of these issues. First, try to find out how many of your customers are unhappy by encouraging complaints and feedback (see Chapter 5). If you do this, you will receive *actionable input* from your customers. Ask them the following questions outright:

- Is there any one thing that we could do better that would make it easier for you to be our customer?
- What is the one thing you think we should do differently in serving you?

Make sure you keep a record of the input customers provide, then ensure you make the changes that they suggest. It is important not to become defensive and try to explain why you do the things you do. Never fight or argue with a customer when they are giving you negative feedback about mistakes or errors that they have experienced while doing business with you and your staff—even if you totally disagree with them. You need your customers to give *you* information.

You need to manage the complaint or negative feedback *efficiently*—which means quickly, and *effectively*—which means creating an outcome that makes the customer happy. Turn a negative incident into an opportunity for your customer to conduct a campaign of good word-of-mouth advertising about how well you handled the complaint. This is the cheapest and most effective advertising there is, so use it as much as possible.

Why don't we complain about bad service?

Think about the times you've been a customer over the past two months. Remember when you were unhappy about any service you received, whether it was buying a coffee or a pair of shoes, paying a utilities bill or buying petrol. Did you express your unhappiness or make a complaint? If you *did* complain, were you happy with the way your issue was handled by the business concerned?

This is an interesting exercise to conduct in a room full of people. Usually, about 60 per cent of the people in the room have received less than satisfactory service. Of them, only about 30 per cent have actually made a complaint, and of that 30 per cent, only 20 per cent were satisfied with the way the business managed their complaint. So why don't we complain more about bad service?

Reasons for not complaining include:

- fear of retribution (chefs spitting in the food before re-serving);
- can't be bothered;
- have tried to before but it's no use;
- it takes too much time;
- the effort is too great;
- staff are too rude;
- nothing will be done about the complaint;
- the business not taking any notice;
- preferring to take business elsewhere.

As customers, we can often see that the businesses which don't give good service also frequently fail to respond well to complaints.

Making sure your customers complain

If you can relate to any of these points, examine your business for evidence that your customers may feel the same way about raising an issue with you and your staff. A further step is to ensure that no customer ever feels that way about *your* business. You need that information. If you let the customer walk out the door without letting you know where mistakes and errors have occurred, you can't deal with their dissatisfaction—and that means you lose the opportunity to *effectively resolve the complaint.*

Managing the complaint

As discussed in Chapter 5, customers base their decision about whether to return to your business on their *emotional response* rather than their satisfaction levels. If your customer is left feeling angry, frustrated or disappointed about the service transaction with your business, they are unlikely to do business with you again. This is why it is so important to find out where things are going wrong in the eyes of your customers. So make it as easy as possible for your customers to tell you if things have not gone according to their expectations.

To write or not to write

Some companies insist that customers put their complaints in writing. This is very bad practice. You should never insist that customers put their complaints in writing. It is your responsibility to sort out your business problems, not theirs! The customer has already done you a favour by bringing a complaint to you. Don't expect more of them. If you insist a customer put their complaint in writing, they will do one of two things:

- They will put it in writing and get very angry doing so (and the letter will reflect this anger).
- They will not put it in writing, but will potentially do immeasurable damage to your business through bad word-of-mouth advertising—damage that you cannot control, even if you know it is happening.

If you need a written record of the complaint, arrange to hear the story at the customer's convenience and record it in writing using the customer's words. This builds and maintains a positive relationship with the customer.

As a small business, you are close to your customers and need to remain so. You cannot afford to alienate your customers by making it difficult or impossible for them to complain. Somehow, make sure you are available to hear the complaints face-to-face at all times.

Process for managing complaints

Managing complaints is such an important aspect of customer service that there is a formula for doing it well. An effective complaints management system must include the following elements. It needs to be:

- easily accessible (which means you communicate to your customers that you welcome complaints);
- very simple (you must have an easy process for your customers to make complaints to you—and for your staff to manage them);
- speedy (have time limits for speedy resolution of customer complaints);
- fair (your business must be fair to both staff and customers in handling complaints);
- confidential (where relevant and necessary—especially in some businesses such as personal services);
- effective (which means each and every aspect of the complaint must be addressed and resolution offered for each aspect); and

- informative (you need to record information about complaints so you can pinpoint areas where things keep going wrong).

If your complaints process includes all these elements, it will be an effective system providing actionable input. This will help in making business decisions about service delivery to your customers.

An accessible complaints process

Your business must *make it easy for customers to complain.* That means letting them know you want to hear if something has gone wrong. Use a prominent sign to do this (see Chapter 5). As well, ask as many customers as possible: 'Was there anything we could have done differently which would have made the service better for you?' Customers will soon learn that you welcome feedback from them.

A simple complaints process

The process for receiving complaints must be *simple to use—* for both your staff and your customers. Many companies are pleased that they receive very few complaints. Usually, this is because there is an atmosphere that prevents and discourages the customer from making the complaints. Sometimes the complaints can only be received by the manager or boss. This puts some customers off, because they just want to have their complaint dealt with with the minimum of fuss by the person standing in front of them.

Mary Gober's three-step method for handling complaints (see Chapter 1) is a good memory aid for remembering how to manage each complaint as it is raised with you and your staff. The Sorry–Glad–Sure (SGS) method reminds you of the three important things you need to address with each complaint:

- apologise and empathise with the customer;
- thank the customer for the information and explain that you welcome the complaint because it provides

valuable information on how you can better conduct customer service; and,

- assure the customer that you will find a way to fix the problem, and tell them how long this will take.

A fast complaints process

Sort complaints out fast and at the first point of contact. As soon as a customer mentions that they are unhappy about some aspect of your service or business performance, give it priority and deal with it immediately.

Some major companies have a complaints escalation department because they know that they don't handle them well in the early stages and need to sort them out when they have become really serious. What fascinates me about this way of handling complaints is that these companies know, and expect, that complaints will escalate. That is, they know they don't consistently handle complaints well. So, instead of developing processes and policies to ensure that complaints are dealt with in the early stages when they are relatively easy to manage, they spend huge amounts of money setting up and staffing departments and divisions that wait until the complaints have turned into multi-million dollar threats to the company.

If you know that you are the only one who handles complaints well, then work out why and train your staff to do the same so that they too can rapidly fix complaints. There's only one key word for managing complaints: fast.

A fair complaints process

If you are running your business legally and ethically, you should not normally have to worry about this rule. However, if a staff member does something which is inappropriate or unlawful, you need to be cautious about being fair to all concerned. Abusing a staff member in front of customers because they have made a mistake is simply not fair. Abusing a customer for making a complaint is equally unfair.

It is important that your solution to any problem matches

the problem, so don't overreact. Find out what kind of action the customer wants you to take.

Don't over-compensate

A friend came to me and asked me to help her write a letter of complaint. There were some minor and important problems with the garden reticulation system that she had purchased and had installed at a cost of $1300 and she needed the company's expertise to fix them.

I suggested she use the three-pronged approach to writing her letter of complaint:

1 State specifically what she requested of the company and what specifically was not done, or not done correctly or to her satisfaction.
2 Specify the result of the company's mistake and error and how she felt about the unsatisfactory outcome.
3 Specify what she wanted the company to do to redress the problem.

My friend did this, requesting that:

- the fault be repaired; and
- the company compensate her with a refund of $100 for her time and effort in attempting to get the problem solved.

Just a week later, my friend rang me, perplexed and surprised. The company had sent her a letter of apology and a cheque for the full amount of $1300. This was much more than she expected and frankly it was embarrassing to her. She neither wanted nor expected such a show of largesse. 'What should I do?' she asked me. 'I don't want all that money because most of the job was OK and I am basically happy with it.'

My short answer to her was that I agreed—the company had overreacted and now left her feeling embarrassed.

> She sent the cheque back and asked them to reissue one for $100, as she had originally specified in her letter of complaint. The company did as she asked; however, before doing so, they rang to say her goodwill was so important to them that they had repaid the full amount. They wanted to avoid bad word-of-mouth advertising which could cost them a great deal more than $1300 in lost business.

It is not necessary to go to such extremes when compensating a customer. Ask the customer about their expectation. Often they want less than we think to turn them from a dissatisfied customer to a satisfied one.

A confidential complaints process

In some businesses, such as personal, para-medical or financial services, you may need to be scrupulous about confidentiality when managing a complaint.

You may also face complaints made about seriously inappropriate or unlawful actions by your staff. Such matters must be handled with great care and discretion. Ensure staff do not gossip about the details of any serious complaint, particularly in front of other customers. If this occurs and the customer discovers you have been inappropriately discussing their issue, you may well do even more irreparable damage to your business, and may face legal action for damage to the reputation of the customer. Keep all aspects of the issue confidential while it is being managed to resolution. It is better to expend your energy on fixing the problem. Then, once it is rectified and the customer is happy, let them do the talking about how fantastic your business was at resolving such a difficult and complex issue.

An effective complaints process

Ultimately, a good complaints process is about whether or not you actually fix the mistake or correct the error that has been pointed out by a customer. This has already been discussed briefly in Chapter 1.

If you honour a customer complaint and handle it well, the two things that happen are:

- You have control over the complaint and can fix the problem that caused it.
- Your customer will tell others about how well you handled the complaint, become a loyal, regular customer and recommend you to others as well.

Effective complaints management also means that *each and every aspect* of a complaint must be addressed and redress provided for each problem.

Often we manage complaints on a very superficial level, dealing with the first thing we remember about the complaint. Sometimes, when I am called into companies to assist with a complaint that has gone horribly wrong, I find that the original cause of the complaint has been completely lost and that the company is trying to deal with the most recent aspect of the complaint.

The following story illustrates how complaints can be compounded if we don't deal with each and every aspect of them, and how we can end up with a difficult customer and an escalated complaint that won't go away.

Compounding complaints through poor management

A woman travelled up from the country to attend a medical specialty clinic in a large teaching hospital. She had received a letter telling her that her appointment was for 8.00 a.m. on a particular weekday. She arranged to have a day off work, organised for the children to be out of school for the day, left home at 5.00 a.m. and arrived to find that some 200 other people also had an 8.00 a.m. appointment! And they were all in the queue before her because they knew about the system of 'first come, first served'. Little did she know that many of them had previously experienced just what she was about to in her day out at the hospital clinic!

By 2.00 p.m. she was becoming concerned that she was not going to get to see a doctor because many of the people who were before her in the 8.00 a.m. appointment queue still had not been seen. She went to the administrative clerk and said: 'What's going on? I've been waiting for six hours.' The clerk said: 'Consider yourself lucky. In some countries you would have to wait six years!'

The woman was understandably shocked by her treatment, and her complaint travelled up the hierarchy as one about the rudeness of the administrative clerk in the clinic. (It turned out that the particular clerk was nicknamed The Piranha because of her capacity to eat customers alive in 30 seconds flat!)

The following elements contributed to this compounded complaint:

- The woman was misled in writing about the time of her appointment, with no explanation of the clinic system of overbooking by 80 per cent to compensate for a habit of 30 per cent of customers/patients not showing up for appointments (failing to adhere to Rule 3: *being open and honest*).
- She was not informed about either how the system worked or about how long the delays would be. There was also no mention of the fact that she might not get to see a doctor at all on that day (Rule 3 again).
- When she sought information about what was going on, she was treated discourteously (Rule 6: *being courteous to your customers*).
- When it became clear that she was not going to see a doctor that day and she had been unable to do any of the business that she had planned in the city during the afternoon (after her 'morning' appointment), she was

told that she could return to the country and that another letter would be sent in about three weeks' time advising her of her next appointment, which would be conducted in the same way (Rule 7: *being helpful to your customers*).

■ Finally, she was very unhappy about the way she had been treated overall.

It is worth noting here that, because of difficult processes, the staff were virtually forced to lie at every step along the way of the service transaction every day.

By examining this complaint about 'rudeness', we can see that several of the nine rules of good service were not adhered to.

First, the hospital failed to be *open and honest* with the customer about the limitations of the system of booking appointments. As well, the customer was not *consulted* about a time that would be suitable for her. She was simply informed via letter of the date of her appointment; however, the letter misled her by stating that she had an 8.00 a.m. appointment when it was really the time the clinic opened for business.

During her appointment, the clinic failed to inform the customer about the long delays she could expect. If she had known she would not see a doctor before 2.00 p.m., she could have gone into the city to conduct the business that she needed to complete.

By the third point, we see the rather obvious failure to be *courteous* to the customer, which is what the complaint later hinged on.

After not seeing a doctor that day, she was told that another appointment would be made for her. Again, no consultation on the suitability of the day would occur. As well, she would again receive a letter about the non-negotiable date of the appointment which would once more mislead her by specifying that her appointment would be for 8.00 a.m.! So she would be given no choice about how best to meet her needs to see a specialist doctor at the hospital.

Of the nine good service rules, six are featured in this complaint. The clinic failed to:

- be *informative*;
- *communicate* openly about the limitations of the system and its inherent flaws;
- be *courteous* or *helpful*;
- *offer choice* to the customer about an appointment time that would suit her; or
- *consult* with her at all.

This customer was made 'difficult' by the system and by the bad service transaction processes. The high service standards discussed in Chapter 1 are, of course, also missing from this woman's experience—standards such as promptness, effective communication, convenient opening hours and positive action when things go wrong.

The second important aspect of this story is the effect of the hospital's processes and systems on staff, and the impact of this on customers.

Look around you and you will see that the service transactions of many businesses, both small and large, are littered with similar stories. When you receive a complaint you need to:

- make sure you have the full story;
- understand all the elements of the complaint;
- understand that there is never a really easy quick fix to a complaint that has many points to it;
- understand that, if a complaint is received, the root cause of the problem will invariably be aspects of your business processes; and
- realise that the aspects of your business processes which fail to meet customer needs in the service transaction could also be badly affecting your staff so they treat customers badly.

By listening to the story behind the complaint you can gain actionable input—problems that you can take specific action to fix. You can also do things differently in the future, so other customers won't have the same experience with your business.

You need to ensure that any complaints coming through your business doors don't escalate. The best way of achieving this is to ensure that all elements of the customer focus code are built into all your business service practices.

An informative complaints process

Your complaints process needs to generate information on which to base decisions about changes to your business processes. Every expression of dissatisfaction potentially holds a key to a business improvement that will ensure customers remain loyal and your profitability is sustained.

You need to know why if customers are leaving you and defecting to your opposition. Many companies, including small businesses, measure customer 'churn', but fail to understand *why* it is occurring. Unless you have some processes in place to know why your customers are leaving you or not returning, you are simply driving your business without navigation instruments.

If your staff keep being told that the wine is not cold enough, it may indicate that you have a problem with your fridge—a problem you won't know to fix unless you hear that seven customers a day are mentioning it. On the other hand, the complaints about your wine may only happen on a Tuesday. Your investigations may reveal that the apprentice chef leaves a wedge in the door to keep it open to make access easier. The complaints only occur on Tuesday because that's the day that the apprentice has the extra duty of filling the cold part of the orders. If you are not using a simple method to record and count your complaints, you will lose valuable opportunities to fix the root cause of the problem.

Overview

Managing complaints to put things right for your customers as quickly as possible and with the minimum of fuss is a critical part of good service transaction processes.

Complaints should be resolved to the satisfaction of your customers—without damaging your business. Mistakes happen in business operations and service processes, and errors sometimes occur. Because you understand this about your business, you can make receiving and managing complaints a low-key but important issue for you, the customer and your staff.

Effective complaints management has two main purposes:

- to minimise the potential damage that can be done to your business from bad word-of-mouth advertising; and
- to satisfy a customer by resolving their complaint so they happily use your business again.

Putting things right for your customers: questions for your business
- Do you and your staff act quickly to correct errors in work or mistakes in processes once you become aware of them?
- Are your customers comfortable about informing you if they are unhappy with any aspect of the progress of their purchase?
- When a customer complains, do you and your staff immediately offer an apology, an explanation and a promise of a quick and effective remedy?

Practical tips for putting things right for your customers
- Put a sign in a very visible place in your business which says:
    'If you're happy with the service we would like to know. If you are unhappy with any aspect of our service to you we *need* to know. Please tell us.'
- Offer spot prizes to customers who let you know about something you're doing wrong which, if fixed, will save a lot of money in the service transaction.
- Ask customers to nominate the staff member who handled a complaint best—and then reward them accordingly.

chapter 9

RULE 9: PROVIDE VALUE FOR MONEY

Your customers' perception of whether your business provides value for money in delivery of services and products is an essential part of the service transaction.

Customers compare the cost of what you deliver and what they have received with your competitors' costs. You need to make them feel they have received value for their money. Your business should therefore deliver efficient and economical services within its resources.

The services and products you provide should be charged for at a rate that your customers agree is commensurate. It doesn't matter whether you strive to have the lowest prices and compete on price alone, or whether you provide premium products and services and your prices reflect this. The issue is that, *in the eyes of the customer*, there is a match between the quality or quantity of your product and the price you are charging for it.

If all the other rules and standards of good customer service are in place, customers will perceive that they are receiving value for money from you and your business—even if they are paying a premium price. Like all the other good customer service rules, value for money does not stand alone.

Irrespective of what you expect a customer to pay for your services or products, certain elements must still be present. They are:

- basic service standards;
- product reliability;

- useable products which do not break and are not damaged on receipt;
- products with a life spanning beyond the moment of purchase;
- any related costs, such as those for installation or maintenance, which are not disproportionately high;
- fast, efficient service; and, finally,
- the right service for each job.

Customer perception rules, OK?

Because it is the customer's perception of value that rules here, the price is not so important—it can be high or low, expensive or cheap. The customer must understand that the price matches all the other expectations they have. If the price is low, then the customer will have a lowered expectation of the product quality and service standards. The reverse is also true: if the price is comparatively high, then the expectation of the customer will be that the product quality and service standards will be high also. If the price is at a premium, then be warned: your service standards must be at a premium level, the products must have the highest level of inbuilt quality and the customer expectation will be merciless! There will be a match between expectation, price and quality.

At the low end of the price spectrum, there will always be some customers who will spend $5 on petrol to travel 25 kilometres in order to save $2 on a bargain. They are what we call 'super price-sensitive' customers. All they care about is paying as little as possible over the counter for the service or product they require. On the other hand there are those who will pay any amount so long as the service rules are in place.

Be clear on which customer segment you want to do business with and then direct your business and service transaction processes to that market niche. Always be informative and open with your customers about your pricing structures.

The premium end of value for money

If you charge a premium price, ensure the price is backed up with superlative service which is unquestionable in the eyes of your customers. This means that all nine rules of good customer service are in place and consistently operational in your business. As well, it is important to consider the placing of your business. There is no point in setting up your premium-priced small business in a generally lower socio-economic area or one where there is high unemployment. The passing trade will simply not be able to afford your product and the superlative service you wish to offer with it.

Premium online service

Of course, if you are setting up an online service and will be targeting people outside the area and possibly throughout the world, then you can set up your online business in any location you wish. Remember, though, the service transaction is the same if you are operating online as if you are serving in a shop. Your online customers will still expect all the nine rules of good service transactions to be in place—and early research tells us that they expect it much faster than they do from conventional business.

Coffee anyone?

There is a coffee shop in Sydney, Australia, that charges approximately 40 per cent above the usual price of a cup of coffee. Business is booming and after just eighteen months the proprietors were preparing to franchise the business across Australia and then the world. They are able to charge a premium price because:

- they provide unmatched, best practice service—and they and their customers know it; and
- they are clear that they are not just selling a cup of coffee: they are selling a premium service experience. 111

Customers very quickly came to recognise the ingredients of their coffee shop business and flocked to pay the price— with pleasure.

So how do you gauge whether your customers are getting value for money? Only the customers themselves can tell you this. However, we know that there are various actions you can take to ensure the customer perceives they are receiving value for money. The first is to not appear to be scrimping on the service transaction. Stinginess on your behalf will be noticed by your customers and definitely does not belong alongside the concept of value for money.

Helping people to be your customers

As a busy person, the key service criterion for me is that I can deal with businesses easily, quickly and with a minimum of fuss. A small newspaper round, of which I was a customer, had inflexible payment processes and would not accept credit card payments of monthly accounts for delivery of papers. This was because their merchant facilities charged them a percentage on every account; this reduced their margins on a product with very little room for making a profit. This reduction by a small percentage seriously impacted the profitability of what was a very small family business. However, as I pointed out to them, had they factored in all the labour costs for the work involved in writing out accounts for every customer every month, receiving and processing cheques and physically doing the banking and checking?

Had they also asked their customers how many would avail themselves of the service if it were available? As well, had the proprietors done projections on the possible increase in business if this facility were made available? The answer to all these questions was 'no'.

We could say that this proprietor was offering efficient and economical services within the resources it could afford. However, the service was not meeting my needs as a customer. I wonder how many other people who lived in the same thriving inner-city area had a similar story to tell about dealing with this newspaper delivery business?

The proprietors argued that, even by removing the labour costs of manual account handling, it still was not worth the switch to providing credit card facilities for customers. They preferred to do all that manual labour because it saved them money. I tried three times to be a customer of that business in the ten years that I lived at that address. Every time, the orders would get mucked about, papers wouldn't arrive, I'd have to telephone to let them know and a host of other irritations caused me to stop being their customer on each occasion. Needless to say, on each occasion I would stop doing business with them because it was just too much trouble. It was easier (and cheaper!) for me to walk down the road to the local corner shop each day and get my newspapers.

Finally, simply because I was too busy to go out and fetch the paper from the local shop myself, I again decided to try to have the papers delivered by them. I had no option but to use this particular business because, with only one local newspaper produced in the city, the metropolitan areas were carved up and delivery businesses given exclusive rights to work particular areas. So I became their customer and duly wrote out my cheques every month and posted them for them to process manually.

In the end, the couple running the newspaper delivery business sold up because it was too hard. Their approach had seriously impacted their profitability.

The new owners came in and after just two months announced the availability of merchant facilities. The notice included an authority for customers to sign so that automatic account deductions would occur each month. All I had to do was fill in the form and fax it to the business immediately.

Suddenly, the processes became very reliable: mistakes weren't being made, and I didn't have to worry about

113

writing cheques out every month. So I increased my news-paper order to better reflect what I wanted (effectively doubling my monthly account with them). Previously, because so many mistakes had been made, I was reluc-tant to order many of the business magazines I needed, or special weekend papers from interstate and overseas.

As well, every time a special offer was available—the latest city street directory, or a special calendar or diary—a notice would arrive on the back of my monthly statement including an authority for the delivery business to deduct the price from my credit account.

These new proprietors trebled my spend with them—simply because they made it easy for me to do business with them. They weren't stingy with their processes and as a result, the business boomed. You only need a small percentage of your customers increasing their spend to boost business volume and thus profitability.

Doing it cheaply

I'm often asked about the really cheap, competitive busi-nesses which compete on price alone. When the profit margins are low, there is even more reason to ensure your processes are so streamlined that you are free to concentrate on making it easy for your customers to buy multiples from you. Only the most hardened, price-sensitive customer will tolerate poor access to your competitively cheap products. Long delays for delivery will also turn many away. It is important to ensure that you:

- make it very easy for your price-sensitive customers to get the product they are after;
- have every possible method available at your disposal to get money from your customers—though cash and variations on cash are best (such as direct debit); and
- have plenty of stock on hand and encourage bulk buying by the price-sensitive customer.

Making it easy

When you are offering a very good, inexpensive deal, you must be wary of only accepting cash or its equivalent via direct debit. Make payment by other means available, because in the end you do get the money in your bank account. In the meantime, it's very cheap advertising if those customers continue to come to you (and tell their friends) simply because you do make it so easy for them to buy from you. As well, if you are going to compete on price, you need to be very aware of what the competition is offering and how they manage to do their business in price-sensitive areas. That means getting out among your competitors and mystery shopping them (see Chapter 1).

The best kind of mystery shopping is often referred to as industrial or commercial 'sabotage'. It's not as bad as it sounds. Observe very carefully how your competitors are doing business and steal ideas. That means watching every aspect of their processes in serving their customers for a low price. Assess their weaknesses; notice what their customers are saying—both good and bad. Then make sure your business does not make the same mistakes and that it copies the good practices. Such service differences can become your point of differentiation from the competition. That applies to everything from selling coffees to supplying industrial equipment. No matter what business you are in, service excellence differentiates you from your competitors.

Value for money in professional services

Value for money is also important in service businesses. We all know that every dentist, doctor, physiotherapist, or any of the paramedical therapists, have all been trained at the same universities by the same lecturers who have all read the same textbooks written by the same authors. So many of us do hunt around for a cheaper price—because we know that the background of all the practitioners is the same.

The same principle applies to trades. All tradespeople have been trained at the same institutions, with the same lecturers, using the same textbooks. So if you are willing to offer a cheaper rate for your services than your competitors, you may well find your volume of customers increases. You must still be able to sustain service to them, however. Cheap is no good if you are unavailable when a customer needs you.

Equally, if a doctor or physiotherapist can't fit you in, it doesn't matter how cheap they are: they are of no use.

The personal touch

Because professional service industries and trades deal with people, your relationships with customers can have a direct bearing on their perception of whether they are receiving value for money. It is important to manage the interaction between yourself and your customers with skill, and in a manner that impresses the customer.

Staffing

Ensure that every staff member (and this includes family members) treats customers in a highly professional way. It is critical to your business success that the people you place between your customer's wallet and your till are the best available to manage the service transaction. I am constantly amazed at how many small business owners tell me about the poor service performance of members of their staff!

I remind them to think of themselves as a coach of a children's sporting team. If a young sports player is displaying poor skills, a coach doesn't sack them or whinge about their skills and problems behind their back. Instead, the coach takes the child aside, and trains them to develop their skills. This includes providing opportunities for practise, modelling the behaviour expected, drilling the required skill over and over, rewarding the child when they get it right and pointing out when it has been done wrongly, and getting other members of the team to buddy with the junior and help them further when the coach is unable to pay close attention. It is no different with your staff. Coach them. However, rather than teaching ball or batting skills, you are providing training in customer service skills.

Never forget that staff and/or family members working in your business are looking after your business, your customers and ultimately your profits! Manage them well to safeguard your bottom line.

It is critical to remember that the staff must be able to treat the customer with the greatest respect and good manners so that the customer feels they are getting value for money.

Value of service experience

Some years ago, I wanted to buy a new refrigerator. I had $1000 cash in my wallet and expected to buy what I wanted by the end of the day. The first place I headed for was a local shop that specialised in household goods. I prefer to shop locally where possible and like to build a relationship with local businesses so that they come to know what my preferences are. At the time, I was renovating a house and doing a lot of the labouring myself. Being interested in how I was treated by staff in shops, I went still dressed in my work clothes and with the $1000 cash in my wallet, looking for a willing retailer to assist me.

I walked into the local store and two male sales staff were standing towards the back of the shop, talking. Neither acknowledged me in any way, though they did watch me walk into their store. I stood by the fridges and started looking at them, expecting that one of the staff would come to my assistance at some stage. It didn't happen.

Finally, after about seven minutes, I just stood there glaring at them, in my scruffy clothes and with that $1000 of hard-earned cash sitting in my wallet. Finally the older of the two (the owner of the store) came and offered to assist me by saying: 'What can I do for a busy-looking girl like you?'

Girl? Needless to say, I was not happy. So I opened my wallet and showed him the $1000 in $100 notes inside.

I said: 'I'm looking to purchase a fridge today and will pay cash. I am looking for someone to give this money to in exchange for that fridge. You are not going to get a cent of it.'

At that I turned around and started to walk out the door. He stood in front of me and said: 'Surely I can help you? This is certainly the store that can help you find what you want.'

I just smiled at him and said: 'Too late. I am not a girl, I'm a woman, and I've worked too hard to earn this money to give it to you.'

With that I walked out of his store, smiling and looking back at him to watch his stunned expression.

This service experience left me annoyed, and it didn't matter whether the shop had the cheapest, best-value fridges in the city—my money was not going to them. My perception of their service completely overrode my perception of value for money.

Overview

The customer's perception of whether or not your business provides value for money is based on several factors including:

- their comparison of your costs versus those of your competitors;
- whether your business delivers efficient and economical services within the resources it can afford; and finally

- whether the customer regards your prices as commensurate with the quality of the products and services you offer.

If all the other rules and standards of good customer service are in place from the perspective of your customers, they will perceive that they are receiving value for money from you and your business—even if they are paying a premium price.

Providing value for money for your customers: questions for your business

- Do you know whether your customers perceive that they receive value for money from your business?
- Do your customers believe that products purchased from you, and/or services received, represent good value for the money they have given you?

Practical tips for providing value for money for your customers

- Ask three regular customers per month if they received value for money each time they came to you. If they say 'no' you need to ask why.
- Ask your customers what you would need to do in your business to encourage them to buy more or to return to your business.
- Ask five trusted and five new customers what service changes they would like and/or need to see in place if your prices were raised—then implement the changes (even if you are not planning to increase your prices).

---

chapter 10

DEALING WITH DIFFICULT CUSTOMERS

When the service transaction goes badly wrong, it may be because your business practices have failed to meet good service standards; however, it is possible that the customer is behaving in an extreme manner which lies outside the boundaries of normal interaction.

This chapter looks at difficult customers and difficult interactions (or clashes) between customers and staff.

What is a difficult customer?

'Difficult' customers range from being just irritable (and irritating) through to irrational, bullying and dangerous.

When it comes to the very small percentage of customers who are 'from hell', never accept, tolerate or excuse behaviour which is verbally or physically threatening and/or violent.

However, do not fall into the trap of treating all your customers as if they were 'from hell'. Many 'difficult' customers are created by systems and processes which have prevented them from receiving the service standards they expect from any competent business operator. They become 'difficult' due to frustration about difficult business and service situations which we expect them to navigate.

Go back to Chapter 8, about *putting things right for your customers*, and examine your business practices or service transaction processes: these may have contributed to the creation of a 'difficult' customer.

If you are sure that you have done everything possible to ensure a positive service experience for your customers, you have communicated openly about your capabilities and limitations, and you have checked to ensure that mistakes have not been made, there are some principles to follow in dealing with a difficult customer.

Dealing with extremes in customer behaviour

As a general rule, I believe we create our own difficult customers. However, some customers require special treatment because they are plainly obnoxious or outright bullies. Their attitude to the service transaction lies outside the boundaries of good manners or normal interactive behaviour.

Under no circumstances should you tolerate physically or verbally abusive behaviour from customers. If it is likely that a customer may become violent, remove yourself from their presence as a matter of urgency. The steps to safely take this action are:

1 Tell them you intend to stop the conversation.
2 Tell them you intend to physically leave the area.
3 Repeat your warning twice.
4 Leave the area immediately.
5 Report the matter to a manager (or the police if necessary).

You must *calmly* and *firmly* say to the customer: 'I will not tolerate you speaking to me/behaving towards me in such a manner and *I am now going to leave the room*'. You need to warn the customer three times in total because if they are behaving in an irrational manner, they will not hear you the first or even second time.

Under no circumstances should you stay in the service area and enter into any kind of discussion or debate about the matter with a potentially dangerous customer. Your safety is more important than anything else at this point.

If you are dealing with a customer on the telephone, say the same thing but specify that you are going to put the phone down.

Once you have disengaged from the potentially violent or threatening customer, you need to seek assistance. If you are the owner, contact the police. If you are a staff member, get in contact with the owner or manager as a matter of urgency and let them know that you have left the service area unattended. Remember, your own safety is the most important issue in this case. Respect it.

This is not an experience you should face more than once unless you are in a particularly sensitive service area such as counselling people with psychological problems. If it is happening regularly, you need to work on your business. Examine what you might not be doing and change your practices so you don't anger your customers so much.

What makes a customer difficult?

'Difficult' customers see things differently from you. Look at Figure 10.1. The two people have totally different perceptions of the situation.

Figure 10.1: What does each person see?

Person A sees a 6 on the ground, whereas person B sees a 9. They are both right. It is their perspective which influences their perception. When a customer is being difficult, they are asserting your business is providing them with a '6' when you think you are giving them a '9'.

The first rule in managing difficult customers effectively is to recognise this difference in perspective. Because it is your business, it is your responsibility to understand the customer's perspective—not the other way around. Do this by trying to stand on the customer's side of the counter in a non-judgemental way. Then try to work out what is missing in the customer's information frame so that you can provide the necessary information to help them understand. This may also show you that you have made a mistake and need to fix it.

Difficult situations and conflict

All interactions go through the following stages:

- *Forming*—restrained and polite first contact where you greet the customer and work to find out what is wrong if they seem unhappy or are complaining.
- *Storming*—when the customer displays resistance because you don't appear to understand their complaint; and when you or your staff display resistance to what the customer is saying because you are trying to defend yourself, your staff and your business practices.
- *Norming*—when things are working out and you and the customer are able to calmly discuss all the elements of the complaint.
- *Performing*—when you and/or your staff work hard to find a resolution to the problem—a resolution to satisfy the customer.

When a 'difficult' customer arrives at your business with an issue to raise, the interaction often moves straight into the 'storming' phase. It is this phase that we need to manage. It is very difficult to manage customers who go straight into storming because it catches us off guard.

It takes great skill and professionalism on your behalf to turn such a circumstance around and move the interaction in to the 'norming' phase. But understand that it is *your* responsibility, not the customer's, to demonstrate that skill.

You need to reach the performing stage as quickly as possible so you can understand the differences between you and the customer.

Stress

Stress plays a part in creating difficult customers, particularly the form known as *distress*. Someone experiencing distress exhibits extreme behaviour which may include crying, shouting and violence. If a customer is distressed, they require special treatment, described earlier in this chapter. If you or your staff are distressed, on the other hand, you should remove them and/or yourself from the presence of the customer *immediately*.

When someone has reached a stage where they are over-reacting to everything, they are experiencing *hyperstress*. It can be observed in some very stressful workplaces where the systems and processes prevent staff from giving good service. Such circumstances often create 'difficult' customers. Staff who have reached this stage of dysfunction need to be given a break from customer service.

Functioning effectively

The best option for dealing with a difficult customer is to recognise the threat they present and manage it in such a way that both the customer and the business do not suffer.

This means responding in a way that ensures the best outcome for all concerned—even if this means a controlled 'flight' response. By working in the functional mode we:

- avoid being sucked into the behaviour of the customer;
- remain emotionally detached so that we can objectively examine the facts before us;
- are able to work with the customer to resolve the problems and find solutions; and
- can think clearly about the best way to respond.

Winning with customer conflict

Another helpful model for dealing with customer conflict is the *win/win* or *win/lose model*. This maintains there are four types of response:

- *Aggressive*—I win, you lose behaviour.
- *Passive*—I lose, you win behaviour.
- *Manipulative*—I'll let you think you have won behaviour.
- *Assertive*—I win, you win, behaviour.

The assertive response is the one to aim for in your business when dealing with difficult customers. Adopt a win/win position as soon as possible in every interaction with a difficult customer.

Customers always win

You can see from this model that the 'I win/you lose' position is an excellent recipe for conflict unless one party moves their position. As repeated throughout this book, it is *your* responsibility to do this.

You can never be sure whether the customer is confronting you to win at any cost. However, it's important to remember that a business never wins if the customer loses in any way. You must aim for the assertive 'win/win' model of behaviour that is flexible and provides solutions to conflict.

Many customers will adopt a manipulative 'I'll let you think that you've won' attitude. If that happens, the customer has the ultimate power over the conflict and can do real and commercial damage to your business through bad word-of-mouth advertising. When you let a customer manage a conflict situation in any way other than the 'I win/you win' way, you and your business will lose—if not immediately, then in the long term.

Overview

When the service transaction goes badly wrong, it is important to understand what to do.

While difficult customers are generally created by poor customer service practices, some customers can simply be 'bad' or 'mad'. Before labelling any customer 'difficult', check your service transaction processes.

Never tolerate behaviour which is threatening. Warn the customer three times, then leave the service area or put the telephone down.

Customers generally become difficult because their perception of the situation differs from yours. It is up to you, as the proprietor of the business, to see things from their point of view.

Understand the various stages of customer interactions so you can move the situation to one where a positive outcome is possible. This means getting the interaction to a 'performing' or 'win/win' position.

Remember that the best way to deal with a difficult customer is to manage the situation in a way that ensures the best outcome for all concerned. The business will always lose if the customer does not win.

appendix

CUSTOMER FEEDBACK FORM

[Insert here the name of your company and/or the section/department about which you want feedback from customers.]

Please tick the box which best matches your response.

**Good customer service rule 1:
Provide high standards of service**

1. If anything went wrong, the staff apologised immediately:

Always   Mostly   Sometimes   Rarely   Never   Don't know
☐   ☐   ☐   ☐   ☐   ☐

Comment: _____

_____

2. The business was open at a time/s that suited me and which was convenient for me:

Always   Mostly   Sometimes   Rarely   Never   Don't know
☐   ☐   ☐   ☐   ☐   ☐

Comment: _____

_____

3. I was served by the person who knew about my special needs without experiencing any inconvenience:

Always   Mostly   Sometimes   Rarely   Never   Don't know
☐   ☐   ☐   ☐   ☐   ☐

Comment: _____

4. *I was able to contact the* _____ *[insert] when I needed to:*

Always   Mostly   Sometimes   Rarely   Never   Don't know
□   □   □   □   □   □

Comment: _____
_____

5. *[Insert a question here that is relevant to your business:]*
_____
_____

Always   Mostly   Sometimes   Rarely   Never   Don't know
□   □   □   □   □   □

Comment: _____
_____

Good customer service rule 2: Provide information to your customers

1. *Full, accurate information about the services provided was readily available in plain language:*

Always   Mostly   Sometimes   Rarely   Never   Don't know
□   □   □   □   □   □

Comment: _____
_____

2. *Service costs were clearly stated so I could understand them— and they didn't vary from the quote:*

Always   Mostly   Sometimes   Rarely   Never   Don't know
□   □   □   □   □   □

Comment: _____
_____

Good customer service rule 3:
Be open and honest with your customers

1. I was kept informed of any changes to promises about service delivery:

Always   Mostly   Sometimes   Rarely   Never   Don't know
☐   ☐   ☐   ☐   ☐   ☐

Comment: _____

_____

2. I was clearly informed of any delays in providing service to me as they occurred:

Always   Mostly   Sometimes   Rarely   Never   Don't know
☐   ☐   ☐   ☐   ☐   ☐

Comment: _____

_____

3. I was clearly informed of anything that the staff/business could not do for me:

Always   Mostly   Sometimes   Rarely   Never   Don't know
☐   ☐   ☐   ☐   ☐   ☐

Comment: _____

_____

4. [Insert a question here that is relevant to your business:]

_____

Always   Mostly   Sometimes   Rarely   Never   Don't know
☐   ☐   ☐   ☐   ☐   ☐

Comment: _____

_____

Good customer service rule 4: Provide choice to your customers

1. I was given choice about how I could receive the product/service I was purchasing:

Always   Mostly   Sometimes   Rarely   Never   Don't know
☐   ☐   ☐   ☐   ☐   ☐

Comment: _____

_____

Good customer service rule 5: Consult with your customers

1. I felt I was asked about my preferences during the sale/business:

Always   Mostly   Sometimes   Rarely   Never   Don't know
☐   ☐   ☐   ☐   ☐   ☐

Comment: _____

_____

2. [Insert a question here that is relevant to your business:]

_____

_____

Always   Mostly   Sometimes   Rarely   Never   Don't know
☐   ☐   ☐   ☐   ☐   ☐

Comment: _____

Good customer service rule 6: Be courteous to your customers

1. Staff were courteous in their dealings with me:

Always   Mostly   Sometimes   Rarely   Never   Don't know
☐   ☐   ☐   ☐   ☐   ☐

Comment: _____

_____

2. Staff acknowledged me immediately on entering the store/business:

Always   Mostly   Sometimes   Rarely   Never   Don't know
☐   ☐   ☐   ☐   ☐   ☐

Comment: _____

_____

3. The staff wore visible, easy-to-read identity name tags at all times:

Always   Mostly   Sometimes   Rarely   Never   Don't know
☐   ☐   ☐   ☐   ☐   ☐

Comment: _____

_____

4. Staff thanked me for choosing to do business with their company:

Always   Mostly   Sometimes   Rarely   Never   Don't know
☐   ☐   ☐   ☐   ☐   ☐

Comment: _____

Good customer service rule 7: Be helpful to your customers

1. Staff helped me understand the processes involved in providing service to me:

Always   Mostly   Sometimes   Rarely   Never   Don't know
☐   ☐   ☐   ☐   ☐   ☐

Comment: _____

_____

2. Staff explained how they could help in other ways:

Always   Mostly   Sometimes   Rarely   Never   Don't know
☐   ☐   ☐   ☐   ☐   ☐

Comment: _____

_____

3. Staff did extra things to help me find/access what I needed:

Always   Mostly   Sometimes   Rarely   Never   Don't know

☐   ☐   ☐   ☐   ☐   ☐

Comment: _____

_____

Good customer service rule 8:
Put things right for your customers

1. The staff acted quickly to correct errors in work or mistakes in processes:

Always   Mostly   Sometimes   Rarely   Never   Don't know

☐   ☐   ☐   ☐   ☐   ☐

Comment: _____

_____

2. I felt comfortable informing the staff if I was unhappy with any aspect of the progress of my purchase/business/_____[other?]:

Always   Mostly   Sometimes   Rarely   Never   Don't know

☐   ☐   ☐   ☐   ☐   ☐

Comment: _____

_____

Good customer service rule 9:
Provide value for money

1. I believe I received service and products which were worth the amount of money I paid:

Always   Mostly   Sometimes   Rarely   Never   Don't know

☐   ☐   ☐   ☐   ☐   ☐

Comment: _____

_____

2. Staff thanked me for pointing out any aspect of the service that did not meet my expectations:

Always   Mostly   Sometimes   Rarely   Never   Don't know
☐   ☐   ☐   ☐   ☐   ☐

Comment: _____

_____

Other questions

1. The one thing that our business most needs to improve is:

_____

_____

2. The worst thing our business/staff did was:

_____

_____

3. The best thing our business/staff did was:

_____

_____

Thank you for helping us know how to better serve you.

[Insert your business logo and contact details here.]

Index